THE FEMALE GAZE

ESSAYS ON GENDER, SOCIETY AND MEDIA

DR SHOMA A CHATTERJI

Vitasta
LET KNOWLEDGE SPREAD

Published by
Renu Kaul Verma
Vitasta Publishing Pvt Ltd
2/15, Ansari Road, Daryaganj
New Delhi-110 002
info@vitastapublishing.com

ISBN 978-93-90961-03-0
© Shoma A Chatterji
First Edition 2021
Second Reprint 2023

MRP ₹595

All Rights Reserved.
No part of this publication may be reproduced, stored in a retrieval system, or transmitted in any form, or by any means—electronic, mechanical, photocopying, recording or otherwise—without the prior permission of the publisher. Opinions expressed in this book are the authors' own. The publisher is in no way responsible for these.

Cover and layout by Somesh Kumar Mishra
Edited by Manjula Lal, Alisha Verma
Printed by Chaman Enterprises, New Delhi

To

All my journalist friends, young and old, veterans and newbies, men and women, across language, geography and culture who have encouraged me when I was down, praised me when they felt I have achieved something, stood behind, beside and before me to support, help and guide now and forever.

And to the Editors of newspapers, online journals and papers of all the books I have penned till now.

CONTENTS

Acknowledgement	ix
Foreword	xiii
Preface	xvii

Introduction	1
THE HOME	**7-98**
Same Work No Gains	8
Economic Evaluation Of Housework	13
On HIV, Marriages And Happily Ever Afters	20
Caged And Abandoned	25
The Culture Of Invisible Violence	29
Barely Alive: Widows Of Dead Farmers	35

Are We Refugees?	41
The Deafening Sound Of Silence	47
Of Lipsticks And Masks	53
Domestic Trafficking	58
Monetary Compensation For Rape Victims	64
Family Planning And Gender Bias	69
Should Men Take Responsibility To Stop Violence Against Women?	80
Ageing: A Positive Approach	84
Journey Of A Woman Priestess	90
Is The Prostitute Not A 'Worker'?	94

THE WORLD 99-197

Women And Parliament	100
Women And Regional Journalism	106
Women, War And Conflict Journalism	111
On Gender, Media And Human Rights	119
The Gender Revolution In Film Posters: From Mother India To Kahaani	126
My Choice Or No Choice?	130
When Reel Meets Real: Gulab Gang Vs Gulabi Gang	136
Saankal: A Bizarre Tale Of A Social Custom	141
Mai Ghat: Crime Number 103/2005	147

The Housewife As A Prostitute	152
How Brutal Is Patriarchy?	157
Films In Which Women Dominate	164
Daughters Of Clay	170
Sex Or Gender?	175
Run Kalyani	180
Ajji: A Mirror To System	186
Thappad: A Slap On Society	192

ACKNOWLEDGEMENT

"Thank You" other than "Sorry" is the most problematic phrase in the English language. It has elasticity that stretches anywhere between gratitude and insult on one hand and the fluidity of meaning different things to different people at different times and places depending on one's relationship with them at any given point of time on the other. Yet, it is a phrase one uses almost out of reflex, knowing that perhaps it does not mean anything and perhaps, it means everything. Taking the liberty of the latter—'everything', the author sets forth to use the phrase 'thank you' at its ideal, emotional and most honest hoping that it will be accepted in the spirit in which it has been expressed.

First of all, my deep gratitude to Renu Kaul Verma, Managing Director of Vitasta Publications who decided to publish my collection on gender and cinema the second time round with the Vitasta Publications. I hope she will find her faith in me as a journalist and author fulfilled in the pages of this book. I wrote this book during the lockdown last year and it helped keep me away from depression. For that, I owe it to her and her entire editorial team.

I thank all my editors who published the reviews and articles on issues and subjects I wrote about. Among them are the editors of erstwhile *SCREEN* which I contributed to for 32 long years, Karan Bali of www.upperstall.com, Sujoy Dhar and Ranjita Biswas of www.TWFIndia.com, Sashi Nair of *Vidura*, quarterly magazine published by the Press Institute of India, Editor of *Kerala Media Academy*, Seema Mustafa of www.thecitizen.in, Seema Sachdev of *The Tribune*, Chandigarh, Rajeev Pai of Cinestaan. com, Ketan Tanna of *The Free Press Journal*, Mumbai, Mathures Pal, Michael Flannery and Gopali Banerjee of *The Statesman*, Kolkata, Anuradha Dhareshwar of *One India One People* and many more. These reviews and essays formed the skeleton of much of my analyses that have gone into this book. But I added flesh to almost all of the essays that have gone in this book to update them and render them topical.

I want to offer my heartfelt thanks to my dear friend Dr Sanjukta Dasgupta for writing the beautiful foreword to this book.

I must extend my emotional and moral thanks to my husband, Ajoy for just being there, allowing me my space, and for tolerating a workaholic wife like me for more than five decades and remaining in the background when the wife needs to be out there in the front.

20-year-old Ishaan, our grandson, makes his round-the-clock know-it-allness worth the while by leaving behind a vacuum for us to cope with when he goes home to his parents. Much of the relief comes from him.

My late parents, Asoka Ganguly and Sumita Ganguly cannot be thanked because parents deserve to be remembered and loved, not thanked. But I can never forget their bringing us up in a culturally rich environment of a Bombay soaked in cinema, theatre and literature ranging from Marx, Tagore to New Theatres and Pankaj Mullick.

They taught us the meaning of being Indian first and then Bengali though we were born and brought up far away from Bengali language, culture and geography. They shaped the mould we needed to just pour ourselves into, to become good, informed and creative human beings. Whether we poured ourselves into that mould or went out of shape while growing up is for the world out there to decide.

Last, but never the least, I extend a thanks in advance to all my readers who may want to read this book and perhaps find new windows opening up with each article. That will be the fulfillment of my writing.

Thank You.

FOREWORD

It is a truth that is overtly or covertly acknowledged that from the epics to the epicentre of contemporary popular culture, Indian women remain the second sex, trapped in the triple bind of religion, patriarchy and capitalism.

For any cultural commentator the issue of Gender Perspectives on the question of identities raises in turn one crucial question—the viability of a homogeneous identity for Indian womanhood. Can there be just one definition of the Indian woman irrespective of class, caste and religion in such a vibrant pluralistic society? Indian literature and diverse media representations through the centuries have represented the journey of the Indian woman in her search of the self—focusing on her negotiations with her subjective identity as well as her experiential social participation in her role playing at home and in the world.

Shoma A Chatterji's *The Female Gaze: Essays on Gender, Society and Media* has explored the complex journey of Indian women in the era of globalization and its resultant impact on cultural values and the lives of Indian women in the twenty-first century. The roles of the women have been brilliantly critiqued by Shoma A Chatterji, who is a creative writer, freelance journalist, an awarded film critic and a cultural commentator who is empathetic and unbiased.

It is therefore inevitable that one needs to examine the roles of masculinity and patriarchy for both have systematically contributed to the retardation of the process of gender equality and the ardent appeal of Indian women desirous of claiming subjecthood. Women have been socially conditioned to believing that self-confidence and assertiveness leads to de-feminization, in both cases leading to social ostracism where a kangaroo court adjudicates that she is either a witch or a bitch. The most spectacular instance is of course the burning of Joan of Arc on the stakes, the severing of Khana's tongue, barbequing wives on the funeral pyres of their husbands, the denial of priesthood status to women, barring of entry to holy shrines, the sartorial rigours and women's bodies linked with their appearance and clothing that seems to attract strange obsessive attention. In other words, it is the constructed image that gains recognition whereas the demand for recognition of social and personal identity is often considered as subversive.

In the 21st century, we notice that India has evolved tremendously in terms of technological advancement and is sometimes referred to as digital India but the euphoria and rhetoric cannot hide the abject condition of women on either side of the digital divide. Rape, sexual assault, murder, dowry deaths, domestic violence continue unabated as is apparent from Shoma A Chatterji's essays in this volume. The essays are divided into two parts. The first part deals with 'The Home' that addresses such disturbing issues as the housewife as prostitute, absentee fathers, wives of suicidal farmers and the ubiquitous culture of invisible violence. In the second section of this part titled 'The World' the short pieces cover a very wide trajectory, from unwed mothers, eve teasing and skin-tone to gender bias in family planning, sex-change and transgender issues and ageing of women.

In the final portion a number of recent films such as *Thappad, Ajji, Run Kalyani* and *Sankaal* have been reviewed by Dr Chatterji with incisive insight.

In fact, Shoma A Chatterji's stellar roles as freelance journalist and film critic and her spirited interrogation of gender issues are showcased in these brilliant representative essays that focus on the roles and experiences of Indian women from homes to farmlands, from service sectors to parliament, from ramps to studios, from red light areas to domestic violence. *The Female Gaze: Essays on Gender, Society and Media* will surely be considered as a much-needed contribution to gender studies, media studies and cultural studies and will be of significant benefit to students, faculty members and researchers.

Sanjukta Dasgupta
Convenor, English Advisory Board, Sahitya Akademi, New Delhi
President, Executive Committee, Intercultural Poetry and
Performance Library at ICCR, Kolkata
Visiting Professor, Jagiellonian University, Krakow, Poland (2018)
Professor, Department of English (Retd)
Former Dean, Faculty of Arts, Calcutta University

PREFACE

The Female Gaze: Essays on Gender, Society and Media is divided into two parts: 'The Home' and 'The World.' 'The Home' spans domestic spaces and social spaces. 'The World' covers professional spaces, the media and the cultural spaces. The chapters are topical but not time-bound. There are frequent references to Indian cinema which widens the horizons of readership.

Home and the World was the title of a noted novel by Rabindranath Tagore. The original Bengali title was *Ghaire Baire*, which translates as 'Home and the World.' Today, both these words have much broader implications than their original dictionary meanings. The same metaphorical meanings attached to Bimala in Tagore's novel, whose life changed against the backdrop of a particular phase of India's struggle for freedom when her open-minded husband Nikhil pushed her beyond the doors of the grand mansion's *antahpur* (inner quarters) designated for women to cross the threshold into the *sadar* (exterior quarters) of the mansion to meet his childhood friend, Sandip who has arrived to propagate his ideology and concept of freedom among the people of the small town of Sukhsayor where Nikhil is the 'king' or landlord.

Home and the World, published in 1915, was later translated into English by the author's nephew Surendranath Tagore (with active cooperation from the author himself) in 1919. The Bengali original was published two years after the author was awarded the Nobel Prize for Literature and the same year in which he received a knighthood from King George V of England—an accolade he renounced in 1919 in protest against the Jalianwallah Bagh massacre in Punjab by General Reginald Dyer.

It is perhaps the best known of Tagore's novels outside Bengal, and received a lot of attention in Europe, mainly due to the wide readership Tagore had gained in the wake of his Nobel award. The controversial nature of the subject matter, in which Tagore takes the opportunity to launch his fiercest attack against the ideology of nationalism, contrary to its rising popularity both in India and the West, was also a reason it drew much attention, mostly in the form of reprobation and scorn, from readers both in and outside Bengal. Another reason for the novel's reputation is its celluloid interpretation by Satyajit Ray in 1984.

Though this book bears no direct link to the novel, it does draw inspiration from the divisions of a woman's life between her different worlds—the 'home' and the 'world.'

INTRODUCTION

MEN AND WOMEN are sexually different. Their chromosome structure is different. From this, an inference has been drawn that women's capabilities, aptitudes, reactions, understanding—generally speaking, their dispositions are different from those of men. This inference leads to an ascription of gender difference. Gender identity is a social construct while sexual identity is biological. The upholders of the male/female dichotomy define men as rational, women as emotional, men as strong—both mentally and physically—and women as weak and sentimental, men as theoretical and women as practical. This list of differences goes on. Having listed these differences, a value judgement is added—all male traits are adjudicated as superior and female traits as inferior. The conclusion drawn from this is that mainstream consciousness in society should rightly be male-stream consciousness and women's consciousness should be subservient to the male's.

Patriarchy in this context is understood as men's unjustified structural domination of women, which places a higher value on whatever is projected as male gender identity. The male gender identity is not only sexist, it is also rapist. According to the *Webster Dictionary*, 'rape is an outrageous violation'. This violation need not always be physical. It could be emotional, psychological, and economic. Patriarchy is a legitimisation of hierarchy, exploitation and violation through which women are systematically subjugated, disempowered, silenced and marginalised. Each single one of these amounts to an outrageous violation of woman's right to freedom. The patriarchal conceptual frameworks that have attributed higher value and prestige to male gendered behaviour have also led to certain expectations. The male species are determined by gender constructions as much as females are. The only difference is that males are determined and defined by privileging constructions whereas females have been constructed as having a lack of certain 'qualities' and being 'inferior' by virtue of an ambiguous measuring rod structured by males.

Women's liberation groups argue that women are oppressed because men have power over them; and that changing the situation of women means contesting, and eventually breaking this power. In its simplest form, the power analysis of gender pictured women and men as social blocs linked by a direct power relation. There have been different accounts of the relation between the two blocs. Christine Delphy's *The Main Enemy*, with French farming households in mind, stressed the economic exploitation of wives by husbands. American theorists tended to bypass economics for politics. Shulamith Firestone in *The Dialectic of Sex* saw a collective power play by men with the child-raising family as its central institution. In this work, sexual reproduction took precedence over housework. Mary Daly in *Gyn/Ecology* pictured a global patriarchy sustained by force, fear and collaboration. Radical-feminist analyses of rape such as Susan Brownmiller's *Against Our Will*, and of pornography, such as Andrea Dworkin's *Pornography: Men Possessing Women* have generally followed this model.

There are other studies that treat the power of men and the subordination of women as effects of imperatives outside the direct relationship between the two. These arguments mainly explore the thesis of the reproduction of social structures as well as of bodies from generation to generation. Dorothy Dinnerstein in *The Mermaid and the Minotaur* for example, argues that the power of men and the acquiescence of women stems from women's monopoly over early child rearing, which has been a historical necessity for mankind.

Modernisation theorists say that women are free to enter and remain in the market place through remunerated jobs, though cultural norms in most societies define the household as the primary sphere of a woman's life. But this very role of the woman as housewife and mother restricts her occupational choice to be in the market place. The other factor that limits the entry of the woman into the market place for remunerated work is the socialised and predetermined gender role of the man. His masculinity is linked directly to his ability to provide for the upkeep of the family—wife, children and old parents. This makes many men stop their wives from seeking jobs outside their domestic sphere because they are convinced that earning for the family upkeep is strictly for men.

Ideology regarding gender categories has been a primary

stumbling block to women's access to resources, particularly land. The designation of women as primary food farmers and providers used to encourage a relative equality and complementarity between male and female qualities; but with changing material conditions the complementary roles played by men and women have become much less equal. The contradictions in women's role as primary food farmers have deepened, and what is evident is termed 'feminisation of poverty'.

In many countries in Africa, as elsewhere, there has been a significant increase in the percentage of female-headed households (FHH) in recent years. Among the main causes are male migration, the deaths of males in civil conflicts and wars, unpartnered adolescent fertility and family disruption. Development initiatives have often tried to direct resources and services to FHHs on the assumption that they were poorer than households headed by men (MHHs) and less able to improve their situation without special help. What recent IFAD poverty assessments show is that the reality is more complex.

The developmentalism thesis, a reformulated form of modernisation, stated that the impact of social and cultural changes is not distributed evenly across all sections of society. A disproportionate share of the burdens of economic and social development is borne by disadvantaged groups such as women, minorities and the poor. According to Esther Boserup, societies in Latin America, Africa and Asia have usurped the productive role of women and have also threatened their well-being during the process of change.

More often than not, women are seen as objects of change rather than as agents of change, imitators rather than initiators, bystanders rather than full participants. Despite legal and constitutional privileges, marked inequalities persist between men and women. In this context, gender review describes the particular kind of oppression that women face in social relationships like production and reproduction. The pressure to adopt sex-appropriate behaviour is proof of how the patriarchal socialisation process controls women in several ways: (i) it defines women; (ii) it defines the external world and the positioning of women within this world; (iii) it provides women's definition of others and their relationship with themselves. This establishes the assumption that the determinant factor of a woman's identity and her participation in social relationships is her association with man, while her social position is determined by her relationship with men. The concept of male domination is based on the ideology of sexism, which justifies the power of men over women. The extent to which women believe in these precepts of sexist ideology is a reflection of the powers of coercion and social control. Gender relations in society are so pervasive and so deeply embedded into the psyche of men and women that most of us are not even aware of its manifestation.

Feminist researchers have been challenging the gendered notion of 'power over' and emphasising the notion of shared power, of transforming power into a medium for the exercise of responsibility and capacity. The implications of women being excluded from power and decision-making in the public sphere may be what make for the 'women and peace' connection. If there is a female propensity for peace, it may be due to the male propensity to exclude women from power.

The scenario for Indian women across the socioscape–

rural and urban, working and non-working, organised and unorganised, is changing dynamically in every direction, mostly for the better, some leaving unanswered questions. This motivated the author to look into the different dimensions of the position and status of women across different segments – the personal dimension, the social dimension, women and the media, women and cultural representations in theatre, cinema and literature.

The author has been writing on different aspects of gender in Indiain print and online media for forty-odd years. The insights gained into the evolution—or the lack of it—in the lives and lifestyles of Indian woman has shaped the approach, style and perceptions that define this book.

The book offers a look into the visibility and invisibility, presence and absence of the Indian woman within the personal sphere—her position as a victim of domestic violence, victim of trafficking, the housewife as a prostitute and so on, moving over to the social evolution of the woman across genres of life through the participation as well as representation of the woman in the media and in the cultural spheres of life through cinema, theatre and literature.

It does not emphasise on theory and focuses more on incidents and experiences drawn from real-life events and observations.

THE HOME

Same Work No Gains

DIVORCE RATE ACROSS the world is on a rise. Sometimes, divorce occurs because these couples belong to the same profession. Ironically, it is usually the vocation that brings them together in their initial few interactions. It is generally believed that being in the same line of work forges a bond that leads to a better understanding within the marriage. This applies more to occupations that demand more time such as medicine or that have odd hours of work, or are offbeat or unconventional.

Sadly, the schisms in such marriages are easily smoothened the minute the wife gives up her vocation, either on her own volition or by reason of the pressures put on her, or because social conditioning taught her to place marriage before work. Hindi film actors Neetu Singh and Sharmila Tagore gave up their careers at the peak in an effort to keep the marriage intact. Tagore did make a comeback but only after her children grew up. Sometimes, the man leaves his profession too. But such cases are very rare and unheard of.

Medicine, theatre, films, modeling, public relations, politics and advertising are a few vocations that create void between couples when they happen to have a common profession. It takes time for Indian men and women, conditioned by patriarchy over hundreds of years, to cope with the woman rising above her husband in the same occupation. This is a serious factor that could work against a husband-wife relationship.

Between two academics, if the husband gets a research grant from a foreign university, family and colleagues give him a fond farewell. But if the wife gets the same grant, she often has to refuse it because 'The family comes first.' So, fewer married women academics apply for research grants to study abroad than men because they have accepted that they 'should not leave the family for two years to get a foreign degree and earn some foreign exchange.'

Sweeping generalisations would be unfair to those women who stick to their guns despite being married. It works fine for some of them. One often finds that a married couple where each partner is extremely successful in his/her respective career works well when either is into a different vocation. But if the couple happens to be in the same profession, the problem arises. Each vies with the other for fame, success and power. This usually leads to heartbreak, separation and often divorce or an unhappy marriage. The prospect of leading a lonely life when one is old, tired and desperate for company follows the snowball of wreck already caused in the lives of two individuals.

Pandit Ravi Shankar was married to his guru's daughter Annapoorna Devi, who was reportedly more talented. The marriage broke up, allegedly affecting their only son so badly that he died of the after-effects of drug addiction in the US. He was married and had a son. Annapoorna Devi retreated into a shell, never to step out again. She lived a reclusive life in Mumbai and stopped teaching music. She was married to one of her students, Rooshi Kumar Pandya, who surrendered completely to her demand for absolute privacy of space in their shared life.

Nobel Laureate and economist Amartya Sen's marriage to Nabaneeta Sen probably broke because both of them were academic scholars of high merit. Allegedly, while Amartya travelled across the world, teaching at different universities, Nabaneeta, who accompanied him on his earlier visits, had to stay back, teach at Jadavpur University and raise their two daughters. After their divorce, she remained single while Amartya married again.

Theatre personality Shombhu Mitra met Tripti Bhaduri at the Indian People's Theatre Association (IPTA) when, during pre-Independence, the IPTA was spearheading a movement of political resistance against the British Government through theatre. Later, the two together founded *Bohurupee*, raising Bengali theatre to heights it had never known before. But when they grew old, they lived separately, with daughter Saoli shuttling between the two.

Conflict develops when professional egos begin to overshadow and overpower the emotional relationship. When the wife becomes more successful, famous and earns more than her husband in the same profession, the husband's ego finds it difficult to cope with the reality that his wife is more successful.

This came across in Hrishikesh Mukherjee's film *Abhimaan*. The husband, at the top of the ladder, failed to accept that his wife was more talented than he was. He did not know this when he married her. But later, when she stepped into public life with her singing—egged on by the same husband—she became famous and began to earn more than him. He threw her out of the home even though she had given up taking singing contracts by then because she knew it was breaking her marriage.

Danseuse-actress Mamata Shankar, daughter of the late Pandit Uday Shankar, is fortunate to have found her match in Chandroday Ghosh, a qualified engineer who gave up his profession completely to take on the management of his wife's dance troupe and dance schools spread in different parts of West Bengal. He also took professional lessons in classical Indian dance and choreography. With two grown sons, the Shankars are living happily together.

Kishore and Rita Bhimani are both linked to the media. While Kishore was a veteran journalist, wife Rita is a high-profile public relations person. With a nearly forty-year-old marriage behind them, the couple did not seem to suffer from ego problems. 'Both are very successful in their respective careers. Maybe, the fact that they did not harbour ego problems was the reason for their success in professional and in personal life,' said a close friend of the Bhimanis.

'If we accept our professions for whatever they are worth and manage to keep them out of our personal life, such problems need not arise at all,' says Kheyali Dostidar, a stage and television actress married to another media personality, Arindam Ganguly. 'Arindam and I have worked out an arrangement where we work together on the same project and divide responsibilities between us,' she says. So, when Arindam is producing and directing a television serial, Kheyali takes care of the script. 'There are areas where each of us specialise and we make optimum use of this. So when he is working on the music of a project, I have no involvement in his work except as a first-hand learner. This helps us learn different things from each other and the relationship works on a different plane altogether,' sums up Kheyali.

Kheyali was earlier married to television director Debangshu Sengupta for ten years and had a child with him. But the marriage broke later.

Ustad Amjad Ali Khan's wife Subhalakshmi was a talented classical dancer. She gave up dancing when she married Amjad with the explanation that her husband's music demanded a full-time wife rather than a wife who doubled up as a classical dancer. Lakshman Shrestha's painter wife gave up painting after she married Shrestha.

One wonders how fair is this to all lives involved?

Ecomonic Evaluation Of Housework

IN THE HEATED debate going on around the world regarding housework, the Supreme Court came down heavily on the government's Census while enhancing the compensation to be given to the family of a housewife killed in a road accident. The Supreme Court observed that the contribution of a woman who looks after her family should not be deemed any less significant than that of a man who earns money by working outside.

The apex court's judgment was delivered against the verdict of lower courts that had awarded a meagre compensation of Rs 2.5 lakh to the victim's family on the ground that she was a 'non-earning' member of the family. If a person's worth is to be determined solely on the basis of the amount of money he or she earns, the majority of women and children in India might find their lives reduced to zero value in monetary terms.

The apex court objected to the Census listing homemakers as 'non-workers', revealing the gender bias inherent in this categorisation. The husband of the deceased would now get Rs 6 lakh compensation. The court pointed out that there was a distinct bias against women in welfare laws and even judicial verdicts though there was a clear mandate for all authorities not to be part of any kind of gender discrimination.

Why should the Census classify homemakers as 'non-workers' on par with beggars, prostitutes and prisoners? Even prostitutes cannot be counted as 'non-workers'. By tradition and by law, the homemaker/housewife is not considered to be a productive worker in the economic sense of the term. Her work is non-productive because she does not get wages in exchange for her labour and therefore, her work does not have value-in-exchange. She is expected to seek her reward in psychological and economic terms that comes of her work providing satisfaction to the other members of the family.

Some economists would point out that she gets 'paid' for her services in real terms—in terms of food, clothing, shelter, goods and services. This 'payment' in return for housework is said to determine her status within the family. But in pure quantitative terms, isn't the work she does greater than the goods and services she consumes? Is she then, not creating surplus value for others to benefit from? If she is creating surplus value, then her work is certainly productive. She does not draw any salary, is not entitled to retirement benefits, does not qualify for any leave—be it privilege, sick, casual—or travel benefits, medical and other benefits, provident fund or dearness allowance. Housework is not included in computing the Gross National Product (GNP). But this in no way means that housework is an uneconomic activity.

Some factors common to housework for homemakers

across the world may be enumerated as follows:
- Housework is essential to the socio-economic structure of which the family is the basic unit.
- Housework is petty, isolated and monotonous involving unending hours of hard and unrewarding labour.
- Housework is highly labour-intensive but is not paid for.
- Housework is geographically, horizontally, vertically and occupationally immobile, unlike work by nurses, teachers, carpenters or economists.
- Housework is hazardous and risky. It is estimated that about 14 million housewives in the US are injured inside their homes every year, apart from being injured in marital violence.
- The basic sex-role definition of the woman's role as homemaker restricts the occupational choices of women.

Is it not ironical, therefore, that the commercial market economy has a financially valued analogy for every item of housework a homemaker does on a daily basis without payment? Restaurant meals provide the parallel for preparing, cooking and serving food. Laundering services provide the analogy for washing and ironing. Housecleaning can be done professionally by professional housekeepers and domestic maids. Crèches, play-houses and baby sitters can take care of small children. These services need to be paid for and thus they are computed while measuring the GNP. But a homemaker provides all these services for free, so her services are kept out of evaluation and measurement of GNP.

In a world of materialistic and consumerist culture, the

mother-wife role for women has been repeatedly and assertively reinforced. The United Nations Development agencies stressed on the maternal deprivation syndrome, offering the World War II example when children suffered without their mothers who were forced to come out and work in agriculture and industry because men had gone to war. They claimed that children need their mothers, who must remain at home and be protected by the men. Margaret Mead attacked this UN theory in 1954 as 'a subtle and new form of anti-feminism in which men under the guise of exalting the importance of maternity are tying women more tightly to their children.' Another limiting factor is the predetermined, socially conditioned role of men which links a man's masculinity to his ability to provide for his family consisting of elderly parents, wife and children.

The disparity between the male and female condition in a capitalist society is the real problem. If our realisation as individuals having 'value' in bourgeois society is only through our roles as buyers and sellers of commodities (or specifically as sellers of labour power and earners of a wage), bearing and rearing children is an obstacle to this realisation. Although part of the toll of being parents can be shared, bearing the child cannot: whatever her class, the woman is discriminated against with respect to the male in capitalism.

Patriarchal norms attribute most responsibility for child-care and home management to homemakers while they hold men accountable for the financial support of the family. These norms:
- limit women's education and training
- lower their employment aspirations
- reduce the time and energy available for extra-domestic work

- restrict women's access to technology and credit

Thus, within the labour market, women participate in an unequal competition with men for jobs.

Women's groups have long being advocating the inclusion of housework as an economic activity. So far no change has been accepted internationally. Nevertheless, without the supporting role of activities like cleaning, cooking and caring in the households, members of the household involved mainly in productive activities will not be able to achieve their allocated tasks. Hence, housework is crucial in all aspects of development.

'The countless chores collectively known as "housework"— cooking, washing dishes, doing laundry, making beds, sweeping, shopping etc apparently consume some three to four thousand hours of the average housewife's year,' wrote Ann Oakley in *The Sociology of Housework,* in 1974. Startling as this statistic may be, it does not even account for the constant and unquantifiable attention mothers must give to their children. Just as a woman's maternal duties are always taken for granted, her never-ending toil as a homemaker rarely occasions expressions of appreciation within her family.

To generate labour power, two things are necessary: one, the raw materials that the labourer buys from the market for subsistence and two, the labour that is involved in transforming these raw materials into consumable items for the labourer's individual consumption that will create labour power and sustain it. The homemaker is directly and wholly concerned with the second and partially concerned with the first. These items of consumption generate labour power in the labourer not only for the next day's labour but also pave the way for producing the next generation of labour through progeny. But this is possible only if the labourer survives and the labourer can survive only if he consumes the basic necessities of life at the right time and in the right quality and quantity.

So, both for labour power for the next day and supply of labour for the next generation, the homemaker has to be continuously engaged in housework. From this standpoint, housework is definitely productive work as it sustains labour power and helps create labour for the future.

Though the relationship among the members of a family is essentially non-capitalist, the housework done by the homemaker and the labour provided by the male members are the basic pre-conditions to the existence and sustenance of the capitalist system of production which has actually created and nourished this non-capitalist façade for its own benefit and survival. Lenin defined housework as 'the most unproductive, the most barbarous and the most arduous work a woman can do. It is exceptionally petty and does not include anything that would in any way promote the development of the women.' Nothing has changed since.

> An ILO report found that if the value of housework is calculated as equivalent to paid services performed by cooks, cleaners, housekeepers and nurses, it would contribute to half the GNP in many countries. Domestic work, says the same source is 'women's work' whether she is in paid employment or not. The average for 12 industrialised countries in mid-1980s outlining the allocation of 100 per cent

time among free time, unpaid work and paid work shows – (a) the full-time homemaker who does not have a job devotes 56 per cent of her time to unpaid work (housework), enjoys 33 per cent of free time and spends hardly one per cent on paid work; (b) the homemaker who has a salaried job devotes 31 per cent of her time to unpaid housework, enjoys 24 per cent of free time and devotes 40 per cent of her time to paid work; (c) the average man who has a salaried job commits 11 per cent of his time to unpaid work, enjoys 34 per cent of free time and devotes 49 per cent to paid work.

—*Recommendation 123: Concerning the Employment of Women with Family Responsibilities, 49th Session, June 1965*

On HIV, Marriages And Happily Ever Afters

THE DEFINITION OF the term 'family' has changed radically over the past two decades across the world. Even though conventional family structures exist, there have been permutations and combinations that demand the enlargement of the sphere of social acceptance. One dimension of this changing scenario is marriage between HIV+ couples.

A marriage of this kind can be of two types—where one of the two partners is HIV+ or where both partners are HIV+. But there are some other aspects that need to be figured in too. For instance did one partner or both know the diagnosis before they were married? Did the illness endanger the relationship after they tied the knot?

These questions are redundant when death is just round the corner and you can do nothing about it. So, how do couples live with the constant thought that they will die soon? Does life become an entity stripped of all meaning? Many HIV+ men and women are getting married without letting their secrets out and trying to cope with whatever is left of their lives with some quality and positive thinking.

Ramakrishnan and Mary got married in Chennai. Both are HIV+ and members of South India Positive Network (SIPN.) A routine medical test showed Ramakrishnan's HIV+ status while Mary had caught the virus from her ex-husband who had died of AIDS some time back. This is an example of a couple that is consciously leading a protected married life. As their children could be born with the virus, they are considering adoption as an option or foregoing kids altogether.

GV Joshi, an activist says, 'In Gujarat HIV+ people are looking at a new therapy—marriage within the community of HIV+ people.' He cites the example of Manohar, an unmarried diamond worker and his wife Sujata, who had caught the virus from her husband, just as in the example above. The two met at counselling meetings and decided to tie the knot. Manohar says that the marriage has brought him a sense of peace because he does not have to hide his affliction from her and she knows exactly how to handle his special needs for high-protein food and regular medicines. 'We understand each other's physical and emotional needs,' they chorus with Manohar adding, 'This is the best decision of my life.'

Manohar says, 'But there are more exceptions to this happy story than one would wish. My family was forcing me to marry a healthy woman without informing her about my illness. But I could not have lived with the guilt of passing on the virus to an unsuspecting girl. It would have made my life a living hell and now we have decided not to raise a family at all. My personal take on marriage between HIV+ couples who have already crossed the border of safety and are destined to die is companionship that helps in fighting the disease.'

According to the Gujarat State Network of People living with HIV and AIDS (GSNP), marriages between HIV+ people may herald a new beginning both in the efforts at preventing the spread of the HIV and the way these people lead their lives. GSNP started the first ever marriage bureau for HIV-infected people in the state. It counsels HIV+ couples to refrain from having children, as they would run a high risk of being born with the infection. But there is a problem because the number of HIV+ young men far exceeds the number of HIV+ young women. Many young sex workers are HIV+ and the social stigma attached to the profession stops even HIV+ men from marrying these girls. If such networks and communities are formed in all states, more HIV+ men and women can get married and lead a happy married life for the rest of their remaining lives.

Just like normal couples often match horoscopes and blood groups, HIV+ couples intending to marry are advised to match their CD-4 counts that indicates the immunity level of the affected person. Once the virus enters the body, it attaches itself to a white blood cell (WBC) called CD-4, alternatively called T4 cells. They are the chief fighters of disease in the body. Whenever there is an infection, CD-4 cells lead the infection-fighting army of the body to protect it from falling sick. Damage to these cells can affect a person's disease-fighting capability and general health. The number of CD-4 cells per millilitre of blood (called the CD-4 count), ranges between 500 and 1,500 in a healthy person. According to an HIV/AIDS specialist, when the CD-4 count drops below 200, a person falls prey to infections like TB, fungus, pneumonia and some forms of cancer. A person with CD-4 count above 400-500 is considered absolutely disease-free.

According to Dr Sanjay Govindraj, an AIDS counsellor in Bengaluru, 'If both the man and the woman are aware that they are carrying the virus, there is no problem if they want to get married. The counselors, instead of advising them against marriage, should help them make up their minds.' HIV+ men can marry non-HIV+ women if the latter are well informed and still willing. They can have a protected conjugal life, lead normal lives, but should not have any children. However, many people are under pressure from their families, especially when the parents do not know that their child is affected and the child is afraid to let the parents know the truth.

The battle against Acquired Immuno Deficiency Syndrome (AIDS) develops in a person who is HIV+. Sometimes, it takes a few years to develop into full-blown AIDS. Sometimes, it takes many years. Shyamala Ashok, AIDS counsellor, Pondicherry, says, 'HIV+ men and women would be psychologically better off if they get married to each other.'

Premilla D' Cruz's study, *In Sickness and in Health—The Family Experience of HIV/AIDS in India* (2003), explains how in some cases, where the progress of the husband's infection has not reached a stage that could affect the well-being of the family, HIV and its implications led to greater bonding between the spouses. There was a greater sense of support and protectiveness between them. Problems increase in direct proportion to the husband's degree of infection when he has been responsible for having invited it by visiting sex workers, drinking, gambling and leading an immoral life. In such cases, she reports that concern, support, compassion and protectiveness co-exist with anger and resentment in the wives. The anger results not as much from the husband's promiscuous lifestyle as it does from the impact of the disease on the entire family in financial, emotional and moral terms. The unhappiness in sex life gets mitigated over time. However, most wives did not express their resentment openly because they felt it would increase the pain the husband was already reeling under.

Love within marriage, as we all know, is not just about sex and having children. It is about a shoulder you can rest your head on, a mind you can reach out and touch, a person who shares happiness and joy with you all your life, and death.

(*Note: Names have been changed to protect the privacy of the subjects.*)

Caged And Abandoned

BEFORE IT WAS divided into two, Bengal produced great men who defined a new renaissance in culture, literature, drama, religion, education, fine arts and performing arts. But few of us have cared to discover who the women in their lives were and how they led their lives as wives of great men. Some sad, irreversible truths are described in a slim book called *Pinjare Boshiya* (Sitting In a Cage) which was published in 1996 in Kolkata. It unfolds the tragedies of young widows who lived a life of emotional and physical torture just because they were widows and in most cases, had been married to men old enough to be their fathers.

The author, late Kalyani Dutta, taught Sanskrit language and literature at Kolkata's Basanti Debi College for many years. She was a prolific, distinguished scholar and was forever surrounded by books and students as she lived alone. She was in her seventies when this book was published and one wonders why no one thought of translating it in different Indian languages. Her extra-mural researches were on oral history of Bengal which also brought forth books like *Thod Bodi Khada* and *Khada Bori Thod* other than *Baidhabya Kahini* (Tales of Widows), most of which are out of print.

Pinjore Boshiya was first published in 1996 but it has tremendous archival value for posterity as it sheds light on a subject of wives in great Bengali families and what 'life in the shadows' meant for them. In her sparklingly informative introduction, Nabaneeta Deb Sen writes that Dutta's writing underscores the decline of the importance of oral history in an era of techno-revolution. Her upholding of the woman's cause does not succumb to the Western influenced brand of feminism contemporary Indian women seem to be so fond of. Dutta has uncovered the fascinating truth of the literary genius of some of her subjects—all widows of the past century or the turn of the present century, some of whom have turned their culinary books into treatises on history and literature.

Dutta's subjects have been drawn from first-hand experiences of witnessing close relatives who were widowed while still very young. Many have been drawn from hearsay and stories narrated to her by her own mother, by her colleagues in college, all of whom who seem to have this common thread of a widowed relative whose life was worse than death. She talks, for instance, about one particular distant relative, an aunt who was widowed at eleven and lived to be ninety-five. When she died, her great-grandchildren jokingly remarked that if she could live so long by having one meal through life, she might have lived to celebrate her 200 birthday had she had two square meals a day!

The title 'Sitting in a cage' metaphorically refers to Bengali Hindu widows who were caged within the most rigid rules defined for them by the patriarchal society they lived in. The period of the book begins around the passage of the Widow Remarriage Act, 1856 till around the 1930s and '40s. Therefore, the lot of the widows described by Dutta sounds strikingly ironical and cruel because, as several of her personality profiles show, many of these women sincerely believed that their sorrows were due to some sin they had committed in their previous birth. Thus, they rigidly stuck to every single ritual that was imposed on them without ever raising questions.

There are repeated references to their practice of fasting on *Ekadashi*, falling the day after *Dashami* of every lunar month. On this day, a widow had to fast the whole day without a drop of water. During a cholera epidemic, if a widow-victim of cholera happened to fall sick on *Ekadashi*, she died because she was not permitted even a drop of water. One pregnant widow, who happened to get labour pains on *Ekadashi* day, delivered a stillborn child the next morning because she could not bear the pains without a drop of water!

There are countless instances where widows who had inherited a lot of wealth and land after their husband's death, learnt how to manage and control that wealth. Soon, they were strongly pressurised by their in-laws to go away to Kashi (Varanasi) to attain salvation so they would not be widowed in their next birth. To begin with, they were ensured of a good monthly allowance and good living quarters with the money from their own wealth. Soon after, however, the money-orders would stop. One such widow who inherited half the *zamindari* of her husband's family was discovered by the author (when the latter went on a pilgrimage to Kashi) in a *Dharamsala* for destitute widows, naked, muttering to herself that she had just two torn sarees and so, preferred to 'save' them for the evenings.

Dutta writes 'I have no documented proof for my stories. They have been culled from my memories, seen, heard and hearsay. But they are all true and they all have one thing in common: the torture of humanity in the name of widow rituals.'

What stands out is that these real-life stories of women's oppression are placed in the backdrop of aristocratic, wealthy, educated and some very famous Bengali families. A few of the subjects, like Sibmohini Devi, were remarried at the behest of Ishwar Chandra Vidyasagar himself. But this was possible because she ventured to walk out of her parents' home with the help of a friendly neighbour's family. The author is not biased against men. This comes across in her ode to Surendranath Tagore, who was extremely supportive of his wife Sagna Devi who took *sanyas* later in life. This, in spite of his wife's indifference and her inclination to spiritualism. Dutta celebrates the memory of Sagna's mother-in-law, Jnanada Sundari Tagore.

One hopes someone will bring out an English translation of these stories of subjugation and humiliation to highlight the changes that have swept the lives of Indian women today. But the widows of Varanasi and Vrindavan, mostly drawn from Bengal, still live out similar stories amidst the debris of their lives.

The Culture Of Invisible Violence

THE UNITED NATIONS' Declaration on the Elimination of Violence against Women (1993) defines violence against women as 'any act of gender-based violence that results in, or is likely to result in, physical, sexual or psychological harm or suffering to women, including threats of such acts, coercion or arbitrary deprivation of liberty, whether occurring in public or in private life.' There are areas of violence within the home that are so subtle, so deeply embedded into mindsets and so invisible that even the women subjected to such violence are not aware of these and accept this as an integral part of their roles as wife, mother, sister, daughter-in-law and daughter. There is no region of the world, no country and no culture in which women live free from violence.

Women and girls, married, single, widowed or divorced, are constantly subjected to emotional violence. Even telephone conversations, as in Ruchira (name changed)'s case, were restricted by her father except if they were for professional reasons. Her two younger brothers did not face such censorship. The movements of Indian girls and women are restricted in terms of time, space, occupation and social networking. The reason given is that it is not safe for girls to move and mingle freely beyond the 'protective' environment of the home. The parents and husband are not aware that this 'protective' censorship is emotional violence. As girls, most of us have been conditioned never to question the restrictions placed on our movement, education, space, occupation, relationships, friendships, dress habits and choice of marriage partner.

Leena's husband paced up and down while Leena talked on the phone, never mind who she talked to. After five minutes, he would send signs asking her to call off because either he was expecting some 'important call' or he had to make an 'urgent call'. After five years, Leena lost her temper and insisted that she would either take a new connection or would split the bill. The cell phone, thankfully, has cut down on this constant monitoring of telephone calls made by women.

At a seminar on violence, a participant expressed how her husband forced her to cut off all ties with her parents' family, not even allowing her to attend family functions like weddings, birthdays and *Bhau Beej*. He would flush down the toilet the sweets and gifts her parental family sent. He did not drink or womanise or beat her up. This is emotional violence which women rarely question because they accept it as a part of being a woman. As if being a woman is a crime!

Sometimes, a woman is sidetracked by family members when guests arrive. She is only called to serve the tea and sweats. The guests expect an introduction, which does not happen.

This is another example of emotional violence. This even happens to high-achiever women and women who are full-time housewives. A noted doctor complained to her friends about not being introduced by her husband when friends dropped in. The husband felt threatened by her being an achiever. The housewife is given similar treatment for the opposite reason—there is no need to introduce her to anyone because she is no one anyway!

A man did not take his wife to social gatherings because 'there was no place in the car.' It took ten years for her to question why it always had to be her who was left behind and why not someone else! She created her personal network and went to functions without the husband. She used public transport.

Ignoring, humiliation and insult can happen for any reason—the woman is very beautiful or the woman is very ugly. In *English-Vinglish*, the housewife is insulted by her own husband and daughter because she cannot speak English. In another Indian film, the husband repeatedly points out that the wife speaks English all the time and is therefore, cut off from her roots! Even watching television or listening to music is restricted for many women, especially ageing mothers forced to live with adult children.

Emotional violence happens when the woman is deprived of every human choice that is hers by right and by birth. Theatre personality Usha Ganguly says, 'They insult you because you are "indecently" dressed and they insult you because you have "covered yourself too much". Criticising your body language, your appearance, your weight, colour of skin or hair, your vocabulary or your culinary skills are a part of this collective conspiracy of emotional violence on women.' There is no law you can take recourse to, your only lawyer is you.

Violence against women is not only a manifestation of unequal power relations between men and women; it is a mechanism for perpetuating inequality. Most housewives, employed or not, do not know how much their husband earns, whether he is saving for a rainy day or for the children's education. Most of them are conditioned to silence. My mother never ever knew what salary my father was drawing. Yet, he was a self-proclaimed Marxist who strongly believed in the equality of the sexes and in women's education! It was only after he passed away and she began to get widow's pension could she guess his last drawn salary.

The main wage-earner hands over a fixed amount to the wife if the wife is controlling the family expenses. The money that the husband hands over is less than the money he draws as his take-home salary. What he does with this 'difference' is his business even if he is saving it for the family! That is why when the male earning head suddenly dies, the wife and kids do not have the slightest clue about his financial status. Instead of grieving, they are forced to run from pillar to post to take stock of their financial standing.

Another wife had to write the daily outgoing expenses in minute detail. When her husband came back from work, he would ask for the notebook and circle the items he did not approve of with a red pen! If the red circle ran to more than five items, the wife would be thrown out with her three small daughters without dinner to spend the night on the doorstep of their flat! Yet, she ran a tuition class for small children during the day. She was educated and modern. But can modernity resolve this extreme economic and emotional violence?

'The countless chores collectively known as housework—cooking, washing dishes, doing laundry, making beds, sweeping, shopping—apparently consume some three to four thousand hours of the average housewife's year,' writes Oakley in *The Sociology of Housework,* 1974. It does not even account for the constant and unquantifiable attention mothers must give to their children. Just as a woman's maternal duties are always taken for granted, her never-ending toil as a homemaker rarely occasions expressions of appreciation within her family. The Census of India classifies homemakers as 'non-workers'.

Married working women do not necessarily have control over their income. The two incomes of husband and wife are often pooled for the family budget. Mostly, the wife does not know how to file her income tax returns. Many women do not even know that they need a PAN card because the pooled income is taken care of by the husband. It never occurs to her to keep some money aside for personal expenses. At work, she is often not aware that she is due for an increment and cannot read her own salary slip. She only reads the total and hands the cheque over to her husband. She does not press for promotion in case it involves a transfer to another city or sometimes, even to a different branch within the same city because this will topple the balance of her household responsibilities as a wife and mother.

We have no control over the shelter we live in. When we are little, we live in our father's home. He does not give his daughters a share of the shelter in most cases. Then it is the matrimonial home of her husband. After husband's death, she is constantly under pressure either to leave the home or to transfer it in the name of a son or daughter. Wherever she lives, it is not her house and she has to remain grateful living under this roof. Even in legal parlance, she either lives in her paternal home or in her matrimonial home.

Barely Alive
Widows Of Dead Farmers

THIRTY-EIGHT-YEAR old Vidya More's husband of Osmanabad Maharashtra committed suicide in 2012 when she was only 30 years old. She has a daughter and a son studying in school. Her husband's suicide was declared not eligible (as a farmer suicide) thereby denying her the right to the ex-gratia compensation. She has struggled through the last eight years and has one acre of land now transferred in her name. She farms on this plot and also deals with the marketing of her farm produce. Additionally, she takes on stitching orders and works as a wage labourer for her livelihood.

Kora Santha, 28, of Nalgonda, Telengana, is from Palli village in Nalgonda district, Telengana. She has two sons under eleven who go to school. Her husband committed suicide in 2018, leaving her with a debt of six lakhs. The family land is in the name of her father-in-law and the in-laws are not willing to hand her a share in the family land. They put her off by telling her that she will get her share when the boys grow up. She applied for ex-gratia which has not been sanctioned. She lives with her late husband's family, works as a paid farm labour and runs a *kirana* shop.

'My husband committed suicide in 2018 and we have an outstanding debt of Rs Six lakhs. We applied for ex-gratia with the help of local activists and have been trying to access this support—I have gone to the local revenue office at the *mandal* and district level several times but to no use so far. As my husband did not own any land in his name, I am not considered as "eligible" for getting ex-gratia' says Kora Santha.

Pamidimalla Kalyani, 34, from Mothadaka village, Guntur district, Andhra Pradesh has two daughters aged 16 and 13. Her husband committed suicide in 2019, leaving her with a debt of four lakhs. The family does not own any land, and her husband used to lease in three acres land and cultivate. As he did not own any land, Kalyani is not eligible for ex-gratia. She works as an agricultural labourer. She is not receiving any pension.

Chowdamma, 62, is a farmer from Thippasandra village, Kolar district in Karnnataka. She is the second wife of late Munivenkatappa, son of late Muniyappa, a cultivator who consumed pesticide on 23 February 2019. She has two children, son Chandrappa, 38, and daughter Shivaranjini, 34 and married. They have two acres and 10 guntas of land, which is divided amongst late farmer's children from two marriages. She has a cow, which her daughter-in-law looks after, as she is too old. The family spent around three lakh for his treatment when Munivenkatappa consumed poison. Chowdamma did not get any compensation from the government because the deceased did not have any institutional loan, as per Chandrappa. Now Chowdamma is too old to work in the fields and too poor to lead a retired life without worrying about the financial burden.

Shakila is a woman farmer from Pallur village of Ranipet district in Tamil Nadu. She is related to the deceased Suya Raj. Suya Raj was a farmer with one and a half acres of land. His land was provided with irrigation from the dominant community men. He was under a big burden of debt after borrowing loans for farming, and committed suicide. His wife, Raha lives with two daughters and the family did not receive any government support. However, the report does not state the relation of Shakila to Suya Raj. But her name is mentioned as a victim of this man's suicide.

Ranjit Kaur's husband from Bhatinda, Punjab, committed suicide leaving her to take care of a son. She is physically disabled with a paralysed leg and an arm. She stays with her in-laws and has no land in her name. Veerpal Kaur, 40, is from Mansa, Punjab. There have been three farmer suicides in her family—husband, father and father-in-law. She has two children—a son and a daughter. Taking up the issue of farmer suicides during the Lok Sabha elections, she contested from the constituency of Bathinda as an independent candidate.

As per the official data of National Crime Records Bureau (NCRB), 3,53,802 farmer suicides have taken place in India between 1995 and 2018, with 85.81per cent of these being of men. Around 50,188 female farmer suicides have been counted into this reporting. A recent study commissioned by the Ministry of Agriculture and Farmers Welfare (ISEC, August 2017) reports that the highest number of women farmer suicides have been from the state of Telangana, followed by Gujarat, Tamil Nadu and West Bengal. At least 3,03,597 women from farm households are suddenly left to fend for themselves, to manage the home and the farm. These official numbers are quite under-reported and conveniently-manipulated, as analysed by many scholars. There has been persistent politicisation of the statistics that has blurred the reality of the situation, especially for women farmers and for farmer widows. Part of this is due to the impoverished and marginalised status of these women, partly because they belong to the largely ignored unorganised sector and because they are either illiterate, or ignorant or uneducated. Dominating nature of the deceased husband's family is another reason as the case studies reveal.

In a National Consultation co-organised by Mahila Kisan Adhikaar Manch (MAKAAM) and UN Women on the 'Status of Women Farmers in Farm Suicide Families' in January 2020, affected women demanded a special support package from the government from this Budget itself. "We find that governments are not doing enough to prevent farm suicides. They are not even extending adequate and uniform support to farm-suicide affected families for the women to continue with their lives, livelihoods and familial responsibilities despite the fact that such suicides are due to faulty farming policies", said MAKAAM in a statement.

MAKAAM is a network that has been working on the issues of women farmers from 2014 on a national level. Various networks, campaigns, movements, organisations, researchers, and farmers are a part of this network across the country. MAKAAM has a presence in 24 states of the country, working towards ensuring that women be recognized as farmers in their own right, along with recognizing their rights to land and other natural resources. MAKAAM has been active in Maharashtra from 2016.

Several women farmers complained about the government not recognising their husbands' suicides as a 'farmer suicide' and therefore, not extending any support to the families, and how they have to contend with outstanding debts. Women also talked about how the land title is not transferred to her even after the husband's suicide. After the death of her husband, the wife faces problems at three levels. Getting over the trauma of her husband's death, repaying the debt, and taking over the responsibility of single handedly running her household, along with the stigma of widowhood due to which she faces discrimination within family, societal and cultural levels. Although there is some attention to farmers' suicide at the policy level, the questions of women farmers from suicide affected households however, have not been given much attention.

"We found that there is a wide variation in the R&R (Relief and Rehabilitation) package given by different states. For one thing, there are some states which do not want to acknowledge that suicides are happening, and don't have any policy to support the surviving women in the suicide-affected families. Andhra Pradesh has begun providing a compensation of Rs. Seven lakhs for each family where a farmer suicide has occurred. On the other hand, Maharashtra which has the largest number of farmer suicides gives only one lakh rupees ex-gratia. Telangana on paper gives six lakh rupees compensation but has hardly been doing so after subsuming farmer suicide cases into a Farmer Insurance scheme called Rythu Beema Padhakam. Punjab is performing abysmally by systematically ignoring farmer suicides and leaving the woman to cope with the aftermath of the suicide all by herself. There are numerous cases of multiple suicides within the same family in a state like Punjab", explained Seema Kulkarni of MAKAAM.

Presenting findings of recent studies that assessed the status of women in farmer suicide-affected families from Maharashtra, Karnataka, Telangana, Andhra Pradesh and Tamil Nadu, MAKAAM stated that one of the biggest hurdles for the women to get on with their lives is the outstanding debt left behind by the deceased farmer. "There is no mechanism or policy in place for the women to be freed up from debt made by the deceased farmer, and certainly not in the scheduled commercial banks and cooperative banks when even some Micro-Finance Institutions seem to write off outstanding debt", said Kavitha Kuruganti of MAKAAM/ASHA. "There used to be a one-time settlement mechanism in the Andhra Pradesh package earlier, which was also used in certain cases, to settle within one lakh rupees paid by the government all outstanding institutional as well as private loans to liberate the woman from never-ending debt. We need such a mechanism to be put into place uniformly across the country", she said.

Farmer suicides continue unabated which also show that the various special packages tried out for these states have not been sufficient to address the deep-seated causes of the agrarian crisis. The special packages have neglected the women from these households and effectively thrown them out of agriculture into wage labour, indicative of the disregard of the state towards agrarian and rural distress in general and indicative of the neglect meted out to women farmers.

Are We Refugees?

IS EVERY INDIAN woman a refugee? This question may sound shocking to that elite group of women who are content in their French chiffons or ensconced in corporate cabins that bring them six-seven figure salaries, busy discussing with their accountants how to save on income tax. Or to women like yours truly cushioned in front of a computer to pen rebellious articles on patriarchy or raise my voice to #MeToo. But basically, we Indian women are all refugees because we are forever living in a state of flux, flitting and floating from one place to another, from one city to the next, from one job to another, from one family relationship to another and so on.

This refugee identity is structurally built into our birth and then, socially and politically multiplied several times over till death liberates us, hopefully. So, we are refugees even before we are born because our parents would have preferred us to be born male. In this unkind world, we are discriminated much before we understand what the word 'discrimination' means. By the time we understand it, it is too late.

The Cambridge dictionary defines the refugee as 'a person who has escaped from his/her own country for political, religious or economic reasons or because of war.' Neither of these definitions fit strictly into the life of an Indian girl or woman. An Indian girl does not need to 'escape' from her own 'country' for 'political, religious or economic reasons' or because of a 'war.' The parameters and the qualifying features are not the same. 'Forced displacement' or 'forced migration' perhaps would suit the situation better.

Even if one were to take dictionary definitions of the term 'refugee' and apply it to women across the world, it would be different but equally alarming. Women and children make up to 80 per cent of refugees or internally displaced persons. Women fall prey to sexual violence, torture, rape, forced prostitution, sexual slavery and forced conscription in war. Women lose fathers, husbands, sons, property and employment in war.

Living life is itself a war zone for all women in general and Indian women in particular. We do not 'escape' our parents or the homes we were born in. But we are forced to leave our homes when we marry only because we happen to be born female. If the home is a 'country' we migrate to a different 'country' we know nothing about. When an Indian woman gets married, she is the worst victim of forced migration because everything in her life must change beginning with her name, her social status, her economic base, her identity and at times, even the way in which she dresses, walks, talks and behaves! But the most violative of all is that she has to change the geographical base of her life forever. This practice is internalised by the family, society, caste, community, religion and even by herself so deeply that it does not even occur to anyone to think that this is a gross violation of her human rights.

This world humiliates and assaults us by censoring and attacking our mind, body, life, language, speech, work, dress, relationships, perspective and ideology. The war begins before I am born—as soon as I take shape in my mother's womb. My mother goes in for an amniocentesis test to find out the sex of the foetus. If I am female, the family forces her to abort me. Two 'women' across two generations are locked in a war situation—the one conceived fights a war to be born, the mother fights a war with her body to stop me from being born. My mother's womb is a war-zone for me. Her own body is a war zone for her. If they are forced to skirt an abortion, they will still kill me, by giving me the extract of the poisonous *dhatura* flower—a common practice in Tamil Nadu despite laws banning it. There are other practices in other regions of the country with different names but with the same purpose: Elimination.

I am a refugee in a public place. When I step out of the house after sunset, I might be stalked, molested, groped, teased, assaulted, raped, kidnapped, and murdered. If I work at an office, my vertical rise in my career might demand a compromise with my boss on sexual favours. If I do not compromise, I might be sexually harassed or thrown out of my job. If I rise without compromise, no one will believe I did. The society is a war zone for me that constantly forces me to seek refuge in solidarity through candle-light marches when another refugee like me dies, or, by resorting to the legal and judicial machinery without realising that it is as patriarchal as the rest of the world I belong to and am seeking escape from.

I might get married in the belief that my husband will liberate me from my 'refugee' status, or seek consolation by joining the growing numbers of a #MeToo campaign. But nothing works.

The late Shakuntala Devi, the mathematician with her gift for numbers, had to fight for many years just to establish that a woman had the right to give her mother's name in her ration card application and no one can force her to put her father's name there!

When my parents get me married to the man of their choice, my consent is a mere formality. I must fight the losing war against the dowry they are forced to give because the man has generously consented to marry me! My husband will rape me every night, because he has the State's legal sanction. He believes he has the right to slap, batter, abuse me till I fight him back, tooth for tooth, or divorce him, only to step into the unknown war zone that stalks the life of a divorced woman across the world. A single woman, a deserted woman, a ditched woman, a married woman, a divorced woman or a widow are all refugees constantly searching for some kind of permanent shelter in life.

I am a refugee of my own body. My body is my enemy. I menstruate every month and that is war with my body. My body is subject to every kind of humiliation, indignity and assault known to human history. My parents who rationalise every wrong they do to my being a girl are my enemy. I live in the constant fear of hidden wars against male relatives trying to exploit me. As victim of child abuse, I grow up with a thwarted mind which turns into an enemy. I must mother children even if I am not prepared for motherhood and I can hardly decide how many in how many years or ask 'why'.

I live as a refugee everywhere because society, the State and the law do not offer me a home to live in. My father's family is my 'paternal home' says the law, while my husband's home is my 'matrimonial home.' My husband bequeaths this home to our sons who will throw me out when and if my husband dies before I do. There are few homes for deserted and abandoned women. And they are filled with rapists, pimps, traffickers and molesters disguised as social workers. As a widow, I might be forced to go on a lifelong pilgrimage to Vrindavan or Varanasi to die unheard of, unwept and unsung. Most of the 33 million widows in India live a life of pity, isolation and penury.

The book *War's Dirty Secrets: Rape, Prostitution and Other Crimes Against Women*, edited by Anne Llewellyn Barstow, opened up a horror story of systematic, sanctioned rape and prostitution among women of Korea, Japan and other countries of the Far East during World War II who were drawn from mainstream families into the war scene to function as 'comfort women.' The physical and psychological trauma of the repeated rapes (up to 30 and 40 a day for some women) and poor conditions (living in three-by-five foot cubicles and receiving monthly chemical injections meant to reduce cases of sexually transmitted diseases among soldiers), estimates that only about one-fourth of the estimated 200,000 women brought into this system survived the war. While the vast majority of these women (around 85 per cent) were Korean, some of them were from other colonised Asian nations and some Dutch women who were forced into 'imperial service' in the comfort stations.

I never have to wait for a war to break out because I am constantly at war and have learnt that this war will never allow me to be free of my 'refugee' status. Is it because I, as a woman, am naturally peace-loving as I give birth, nurture and care for children—soldiers of posterity. Or, is it because the nuclear state of mind that war demands, calling for a suspension of disbelief, is alien to me? Or, do I fail to be excited by media narratives of war, spilling over with macho stories of male conquests, defining a superiority I know is a media-creation? War affects individual women, their family, extended family, group, community, village and wider society. I cannot bear to see pictures of malnourished children, desperate people whose idea of sanctuary is the hell-hole of a refugee camp. I cannot tolerate video clips showing entire villages cut off by winter. I am neither coy nor a hypocrite. My reactions are natural, because these images are reflections of my life as a woman—in war, or in peace.

The Deafening Sound Of Silence

HAS IT EVER occurred to us why, till the switchboard operator was a mandatory presence as the only source of communication with the outside world within an office, the operators were all women? Before the invention of automated systems that made the job of the switchboard telephone operator obsolete, these posts were almost exclusively held by women. The few males appointed were either shirkers or frequently moved away from the switchboard; there were incessant complaints about their rude and arrogant telephone behaviour with callers.

Few have cared to appreciate that the job of a switchboard operator demanded a high level of communication skills and an exceptional grip over the English language, besides decent telephone manners. This is a major reason why switchboard operating was one of the first careers completely dominated by women. Yet, the lady telephone operator has been parodied, often in bad taste, in the media, in films and on television soaps. One important reason why women were preferred is because they talked in soft tones, sometimes in whispers and had excellent telephone manners. This has been a trait injected into the female of the species almost from the time she learns how to speak. Imposing silence on women is one of the most invisible forms of violence perpetrated on girls and women across the world.

However, Karl Smallwood in *The Curious Reason Women were allowed to work as Switchboard Operators* adds that two other important reasons for appointing women on these jobs were (a) that they worked for less money and (b) that they could be easily controlled!

From classical Victorian novels to the contemporary Mills & Boons pulp fiction, many leading ladies of literature are soft, fragile, delicate and tender with voices to match. Every negative female character screams at the top of her voice at the drop of a hat, has a shrill voice and tends to gesticulate madly. Women are more easily identified with these qualities than men, and so are considered 'unladylike' and 'indecent.' Remember Nadira in most of her roles? She screamed at the top of her voice, immediately advertising the 'bad woman' tag even if her intentions were good as in the hit film *Julie*. Manorama is another example and so is Lalita Pawar.

Note that even William Shakespeare made Portia and Nerissa in *The Merchant of Venice* disguise themselves as men before they presented themselves at the court in Venice. Portia pretends to play the young lawyer Balthazar and tells the Duke she has been briefed by Dr Bellario and is prepared to face Antonio and Shylock's case. Why? Because the male disguise would automatically 'empower' her to talk as loudly as any man would while arguing her case against Shylock and defending Antonio. Literary representations of women as ignorant, loquacious and incoherent have produced well-known comic figures like Fielding's Slipslop, Sheridan's Mrs Malaprop, Dickens' Flora Finching and Joyce's Molly Bloom. As Olivia Smith observes, 'If one's language is condemned, no means exist of refuting the charge.'

A woman who talks loudly all the time is often labelled 'unfeminine,' 'loud' and 'crude.' A man with a loud voice is said to be 'manly' and 'authoritative.' A daughter in any family is trained to 'talk softly' and therefore, tends to talk in whispers while the son is castigated if he is shy. These are such casual occurrences that one does not even notice them. But a girl with a loud voice is scolded and punished for talking loudly because it is unfeminine. Terming this castigation as 'violence' might be responded with either shock, or amusement, or both. Why? Because girls and women are expected to, trained to and psychologically conditioned to talk softly, to remain silent or talk only when spoken to.

Another example of gender-bias against the woman's voice is visible in how male film actors are almost immediately identified through their macho voices. Amitabh Bachchan, Naseeruddin Shah, Amrish Puri, Om Puri, Shahrukh Khan and Amir Khan are classic examples of this strain. They do not need to be 'visible' to be identified by their audience—their voices do the needful. Pitted against these bass voices, the only actress whose voice was as important as her face and her screen persona was Meena Kumari. There is no one to take her place today. Yet, when one 'listens back' to her voice, one recalls her as being soft-spoken even when angry and revengeful in films like *Sahib, Bibi Aur Ghulam* or *Pakeeza*. More contemporary women's voices recognisable off-screen are those of actors Kareena Kapoor, Priyanka Chopra and Rani Mukherjee, known for their strong women roles in films.

The proof of 'masculinity' is often signified by a deep voice. This supports and reinforces cultural over-emphases on real, biological differences between men and women. Vocal gender images directly affect the lives of women whose voices are perceived as lacking authority. Women speaking in public often call upon their bodies—especially their hands—to make a point or to support their vocal statements. But this very waving and gesticulating is often used and understood as a source of comic disturbance, thereby belittling and ignoring the content of the speech.

Women are not the only victims here. Male dance teachers and men with effeminate characteristics are identified by their manner of speech complemented with hand movements and gesticulations which again, is a conditioned stereotyping of males in a negative way.

Film actress and theatre personality Mita Vashisht, who attended a voice training course in London says, 'Women tend to talk loudly when in a group because at any moment, they either expect to be interrupted or silenced or not heard at all.' So, they seem to be in a teeming hurry to make their point. D Gradoll and J Swann in *Gender Voices* cite how Margaret Thatcher had to take a programme of voice-training when the broadcast of the Prime Minister's *Question Time* characterised her as 'shrill' and therefore, lacking in authority. She went through a voice training drill to reduce her pitch to 46 Hz, which is at the half-way mark between male and female voices.

Forced silence among women is a manifestation of violence against women, very subtle, absolutely silent, and therefore, more ingrained into the social system where women are secondary. This enforced 'silence' is almost impossible to identify and control, because it is melded into the very infrastructure that divides people into men and women and positions them hierarchically along a vertical ladder with men at the top.

Mary Anne Doane states that this gender discrimination between the male and the female in terms of being loud and remaining silent begins with the birth of the child. She writes, 'The first differences are traced along the axis of sound: the voice of the mother, the voice of the father…the mother's soothing voice, in a particular cultural context, is the major component of the 'sonorous envelope' that surrounds the child and is the first model of auditory pleasure.' This 'ideal' of a 'soothing' voice in a female carries through the growth of the child. If it is a male child, he grows up with the conviction that all women must have 'soothing' and 'soft' voices. If it is a female child, she begins to identify with this 'soothing' voice and feels dissatisfied with herself if she does not 'conform' to these 'norms.'

This piece should aptly close with the tongue-firmly-in-cheek comments of Kate Gale, a writer/editor. In *Why Some Men Prefer Sweet, Quiet Women* she tells husbands, 'If you want to be king of your castle, then you need an obedient princess and you should choose your princess wisely, ideally someone who will follow orders, be awed by your accomplishments and be willing to watch pictures/slide shows/DVDs of your travels and impressive leaps and jumps. She should like hearing you talk and not talk too much herself. She should be willing to give up her name/favourite foods/weird friends to be with you.'

So, is the 'enforced silence of women' in and by patriarchy an invisible form of violence? You decide.

Of Lipsticks And Masks

LIPSTICK IS NOT just a cosmetic; it is an object with emotional, cultural and political resonance. So what do we do in an era when lipstick has been rendered redundant?

With the mandatory mask covering the mouth and nose, the lipstick has been the one object of beautification that women have been forced to surrender during the pandemic. The off-and-on lockdown has been keeping us confined at home, and why would one wear lipstick at home?

Research shows that the sale of lipsticks in the US increased in the aftermath of 9/11. Lipstick is a great stress-buster at a reasonably moderate price. A woman has the choice to alter her appearance, to look brighter and better, by wearing lipstick if she wants to; she can also buy a stick of lipstick within her budget, and in the colour she likes. All of which means that the choice is hers; it isn't taken away from her.

Covid-19 presents a completely different picture. The

choice to wear lipstick is taken away entirely from a woman since masks—and wearing one is mandatory—makes lipstick redundant. Global business transformation firm Red Quanta's research paper on the economic slowdown resulting from the pandemic mentions the Lipstick Effect: 'Faced with a short-term cash deficit, consumers may forgo big-ticket retail items like a luxury bag in favour of a small but still premium product like a good quality lipstick.'

Perhaps some renaming of effects is in order. While lipstick has been rendered redundant, there has been a boost in the sale of eye makeup during the pandemic. This is a bit surprising because eye makeup and lipstick are no substitutes for each other. Each has its own role to play in a woman's life, in the shaping of her personality, and in impacting on her social and cultural life at home and beyond. Social distancing also adds to this intriguing situation.

Every woman who uses lipstick will agree that it makes her feel good. In times like these, she may either look for something to replace it or learn to go without it altogether. 'Whenever I have a quarrel at home or feel depressed, I just wrap myself in a lovely dress or sari, dab on some lipstick and step out. I come back refreshed and happy,' says my friend Amrita Soman, who has just retired from her college job. Now she cannot go out; nor can she dab on that lipstick. So she tries to keep her trap shut and avoid conflict.

In the July 1942 entry for her *Leningrad Diary*, Russian poet Vera Imber, a member of the Leningrad Writers Union, records her flight to the city of Christopol on a tiny aircraft: 'I tried to give my pilot—a woman—cigarettes, but it seemed she did not smoke. I offered her half a bottle of good red wine, but no, she did not drink, either. Then after a short hesitation I pulled out a new lipstick, and this, the pilot could not resist. Smiling and embarrassed, she took it.'

In India, women of an earlier era cleverly skirted the lipstick taboo by reddening their lips with *paan* or betel leaf folded with spices and condiments. *Paan* is a very democratic aftertaste because courtesans, prostitutes, housewives, spinsters, and aristocratic ladies all partook of it. It was once believed to be sensual and erotic. Today, many men chew *paan* as an addiction and so did elderly matriarchs like my late mother-in-law.

But back to lipstick, until about four decades ago, an Indian girl's parents were the ones who decided if she could wear lipstick. Later, after she got married, she would have to follow the dress and cosmetic code followed by the women in her husband's home. She had no choice about the use of lipstick. Still, over time and across the world, the lipstick became a language of protest, of rebellion and of self-assertion.

Its potency can be gauged in how transgenders at traffic signals effectively use bright make-up and red lipstick. They dress up proudly and loudly because they revel in drawing attention to themselves, and enjoy asserting their right to look beautiful. And then there are gay men who use dark shades of lipstick to assert their identity and sexual preferences. The little boy in Zoya Akhtar's *Sheila Ki Jawani*, a segment from *Bombay Talkies*, has an instinctive understanding of the power of lipstick when he borrows his mother's make-up because he wants to dance like Katrina in *Sheila Ki Jawani*.

First mass-produced in 1915 when American Maurice Levy designed a metal case for the waxy tube, lipstick was one of the few luxuries purchased by Depression-era women in America. Lipstick hit its stride commercially in the 1950s.

According to Carole Morin, in her column in *New Statesman*, 'Lipstick has always been a matter of life and death. Lana Turner died with her lipstick in her hand in *The Postman Always Rings Twice*. Harry Lime's girlfriend is reminded not to forget her lipstick by the soldier who arrests her in *The Third Man*. When noted British novelist Anna Kavan overdosed, there were 50 lipsticks of the same colour in her bathroom and enough heroin to kill the street. Kavan's lipsticks may have looked the same to the policeman who found her, but there are a million shades of scarlet.'

Lipstick makes a powerful statement in a patriarchal society where women were once looked down upon if they wore lipstick as it was worn only by those of supposedly 'loose morals.' In the World War II era, wearing makeup sometimes indicated overly-sexualised, manipulated women, as echoed in the words of the uncle in Ann Petry's short story *In Darkness and Confusion* (1947). To some, make-up suggested a woman intimately bound to sex, prostitution, and rape, for whom lipstick signified her regrettable victimisation. But in this wartime picture, there was also the sort of woman, evoked in the words of army nurse Ruth Haskell, for whom make-up in general and lipstick in particular was a sign of female agency and of sexuality that was disruptive of wartime's masculine codes of power.

In Satyajit Ray's *Mahanagar*, the lipstick functions as a signifier of the changing face of femininity among Kolkata's Bengali middle-class, especially within the milieu of Arati, the housewife-turned-working woman. Lipstick creates a bond between the Bengali housewife and her Anglo-Indian colleague, who teaches her to use the lipstick she gifts her. Arati looks at herself in the mirror and likes what she sees. It changes her perception of herself but she uses it without her family knowing. When her husband finds it in her purse and questions her, she almost snatches it from his hand and with a flick of her wrist, throws it out of the window. Using the lipstick and throwing it away are both signifiers of her choice.

In *Lipstick Under My Burkha*, lipstick, for the three out of the four women of different ages, backgrounds, faiths, marital status and education featured in the film, is a metaphor for self-assertion and liberation from patriarchal controls. The two Muslim women do it under the safety of the burkha thereby sticking their tongues out at the forced veil.

Whatever the age, nationality or mode of expression there might be, Lipstick has always come out in flying colours albeit those colours may all look similar to men.

Domestic Trafficking

IN NOVEMBER 2013, 35-year-old Rakhi Bhadra, who worked as a domestic maid in Delhi, was reportedly tortured and murdered by Jagriti Singh, the dentist wife of BSP MLA Dhananjay Singh. According to the autopsy report, the deceased, a native of West Bengal, had injury marks all over her body, from head to toe. Subsequently, she succumbed to the injuries inflicted on her by beating, due to 'excessive bleeding'. The postmortem that took nearly four-and-a-half hours was conducted at Sucheta Kriplani Hospital.

Jagriti reportedly confessed to beating up Rakhi, who was found dead in their apartment in Chankyapuri, Delhi. Rakhi had allegedly been burnt with hot iron rods and kicked repeatedly. She had burn marks all over her body and injuries on the chest, stomach, arms and legs. Her son Shehzan, 21, reportedly fled from Chanakyapuri in Delhi for fear of his life and even refused to take custody of his mother's body.

In another instance, 50-year-old Vandana Dhir was charged with torturing and illegally confining her teenaged domestic help in her Vasant Kunj house. Metropolitan Magistrate Gomati Manocha dismissed the bail plea of the accused and directed the jail authorities to provide psychoanalysis and counselling to her.

Calling the incident 'horrible, barbaric', Minister of Women and Child Development department Kiran Walia said the government would bear the medical expenses of the victim. Walia, who visited the girl in hospital, said, 'She has various kinds of marks on her body and doctor would be able to tell whether these are dog bites or not. But apparently, somebody knifed her.'

Jyotsna Khatry's 38-minute documentary *Sons and Daughters* is a well-researched, painstaking exploration of child trafficking in Delhi for domestic service in upper middle class households in the capital city. 'An unsuspecting employer often hires domestic help from a placement agency. Most of these agents are traffickers. The children they hire are likely to have been tricked, kidnapped or forced into work and nearly every trafficked child undergoes physical and sexual abuse during this business transaction. While they work, their salaries are deposited directly to the agent, which makes the child an operational slave. The employer is oblivious,' says Jyotsna in her director's statement.

She started her career as a filmmaker with Anhad, a non-profit organisation, where her role was to interview, conceptualise and edit films on Gujarat carnage victims and on Anhad's work in livelihood and education in Kashmir. She later assisted film-maker Rakesh Sharma on projects like 'State of

Rehabilitation of Gujarat Carnage Victims, 2002', 'Emergence of Hindu Right Wing in the Country' and 'Farmer Suicides in the State of Gujarat'. Jyotsna won the national-level award for L.I.V.E campaign, a *Times of India* initiative, for her short film.

In keeping with the rulings in the Juvenile Justice Act, the names of the children in the film have been changed to conceal their identity. We learn with shock that Delhi has around 2,300 domestic work agencies. Each agency charges Rs 25,000 from each client and takes away the monthly salary of the domestic servant, girl or boy. The children have no clue about whether their families are receiving the money or not. There is no law to prevent child trafficking for domestic servitude in the country, which makes the problem more acute and insoluble.

Responding to what motivated her to make this film, Jyotsna says, 'I was a film student at SAE Bangalore in 2007 when I read the story by Neha Dixit in *Tehelka* called The Nowhere Children. It talked about the different purposes for which kids were trafficked. I had no idea that kids were trafficked for domestic servitude too. That's when I decided to find these kids and do a film with them."

Why did she base her film in Delhi? 'I used to live in Bangalore in 2011 and after trying to find these children and talking to a lot of child rights activists, realised that Delhi is the best place to make this film. I moved to Delhi in 2011. I had no clue about how funds could be raised. I started looking for a job and found one in Times Foundation and funded the film with my savings. By the time the shoot got over, I had to leave the job to be able to sit with an editor and by then I had no money left, so friends started giving us money for editing. We used an online platform called Orangestreet.in where we uploaded the trailer of the film and people who did not know us gave us funds to finish the film.'

One of the kids who was rescued in the process was Vinay, 13, working as a domestic help for eight years. He belongs to a village Dube Ka Purwa in UP's Barabanki district. He says he would be beaten and bashed up mercilessly but he internalised the beating as 'natural' between master and servant. He subsequently returned home with the help of one of the many NGOs Jyotsna interacted with during her research for this film.

Similarly, Sabina from Bengal says she had gone to Chapra Market in December with Rocky, her boyfriend. 'He gave me something sweet to eat and I really do not recollect clearly how I landed with the agent who placed me as a domestic in a Delhi home.' One day, she finally managed to escape.

Also featuring in her work is Savitri, from Lodhma village in Jharkhand who has been missing since 2002. The last her family heard of her was when they got a letter from her stating that her salary was Rs 2,050 per month. She wrote that Sameena Placement Agency had asked for her transfer certificate and caste certificate which the father sent. Subsequently, the girl became untraceable.

Pakur, with a family of parents, brother and a kid sister is from Loondry Village in Khunty, Jharkhand. The parents, when interviewed, could not even say how many children they had! Jayram, an agent, reportedly took a bunch of girls to Delhi from Salepur Village in Jharkhand.

Khatry used a hidden camera while interviewing Rihaan Khan, who runs his agency at Tughlakabad Extension. The camera closes in on his expensive gold wristwatch. He says they get a one-time commission of Rs 25,000. Most of the little girls and boys do not know correct age. The camera moves to a high-end shopping mall asking questions of mothers of babies about nannies. A white lady says, 'Bengalis are good nannies and some of us take them along to England with us. They all come from West Bengal.'

They come from mainly the eastern regions—Jharkhand, UP, West Bengal and Uttarakhand. Assam and the neighbouring states are also not exempt. The film also takes a close look at the notorious case that made national headlines. It is about the teenaged girl employed as a domestic help in an upper-class Delhi home whose employers were both doctors. They locked her from outside and went away to holiday abroad without giving her enough food and even the water supply dried up. She was finally rescued after a part-time maid informed the police. The couple has been arrested. The camera interviews this girl, discreetly keeps away from focussing on the full face and figure of the girls to protect their privacy and to refrain from any sensationalisation of the subject.

'One thing we have badly missed is to be able to have a very open talk with the employer of such children on the whole issue of trafficking for domestic servitude and how even employers are being tricked by the agents, not treating them as culprits, but unfortunately no employer was ready to talk to us so we had to conceal our subject and interview them on a very superficial level which hasn't worked very well for the film.' laments Jyotsna.

The father of a missing girl from Sundarkhali village in the Sundarbans in West Bengal says that he was deceived by an agent in the village who said the girl would be placed in his sister's home in Delhi. Another mother of a girl from

Sandeshkhali, Sundarbans complains that she was not allowed to speak to her daughter working in a home at Sangam Vihar. Many months later, the girl was brought back to her family. Another girl was brought back by her brother with the help of the police and is now reunited with her family.

'We did not have too many obstacles because everybody helped us in every way, be it the NGOs, Delhi Police, subjects and even the people who worked on this film. The biggest obstacle while making this film was my own attitude change on how footage hungry I had became but one of the subjects helped me tackle that.' sums up Khatry.

Fortunately, there are many active NGOs who are totally committed to the rescue and rehabilitation of these children. Shots show a group of rescued girls being sworn in before training at the Kishori Niketan Rehabilitation Home in Ranchi, Jharkhand. Another shot shows some of the rescued girls singing and dancing at the Mahila Sikshan Kendra in Jhansi.

It is high time for us to start caring about our Sons and Daughters and stop trafficking from playing with the future of our country.

Monetary Compensation For Rape Victims

RAPE IS A political act. In *Against Her Will*, Susan Brownmiller argues that the actuality and possibility of rape has served as the main agent in the 'perpetuation of male domination over women by force.' The absence of a *quid pro quo* from the raped woman has turned rape into a volatile weapon in the hands of men. She writes, 'From prehistoric times to the present, I believe, rape has played a critical function. It is nothing more or less than a conscious process of intimidation by which all men keep all women in a state of fear.'

Women know that the possibility of rape exists. According to the unwritten laws of society, they are held responsible for acts of violence against them. This is a powerful tool of control. To make this control effective, it is not necessary for all men to rape all women; just a few men can effectively carry it out on behalf of the rest.

Within this reality, West Bengal Chief Minister Mamata

Banerjee's announcement of monetary compensation to rape victims is shocking. Can monetary compensation to a rape victim justify the humiliation and violation of her body and mind? Does it punish the rapist and function as a deterrent to rape? On 6 September 2012, in response to the rising rate of rape across the state, Banerjee said that 'genuine' rape victims would be paid Rs 30,000 as compensation, if they were minor, Rs 20,000 if they were adult, Rs 50,000, if the victim suffered from 80 per cent disability, Rs 20,000 for 40-80 per cent disability. In case the victim died during the assault, her family would be paid a compensation of two lakh!

How can the CM of a state, a woman, even imagine that monetary compensation would make good the humiliation and physical violence committed on the rape victim? The CM is silent about how the rapist will be caught, tried and punished. She does not say anything about what measuring rod or which machinery of the health ministry will decide on the 'percentage' of disability. But most importantly, her lack of empathy for rape victims in her own state is appalling.

In a poverty-stricken country like India, monetary compensation can act like the proverbial bone thrown in front of the hungry dog. Rape cases will now be 'manipulated' by impoverished families to get hold of the compensation money. Minor girls might be done away with for the two lakh compensation by their families in an environment where female foeticide and female infanticide is an everyday affair! The CM has not explained what she means by 'genuine', or, who will test the 'genuineness' of a complaint.

In 2002, the Delhi High Court quashed the rape case against one Manoj Kumar after the victim submitted an affidavit saying that she was willing to marry the rapist. In another case on 7 September 2003, a 23-year-old Delhi nurse of Shanti Mukand Hospital was raped, her right eye gouged out, her left eye badly wounded by a ward boy. In an application to the court, the rapist Bhura proposed marriage. His argument was that since no one would marry her due to social stigma, he would like to do so. She turned down the proposal as bogus, horrible and audacious.

'He made it sound like a favour. This was more shocking than the proposal itself. The horrible thing in the whole business was the court admitting such an application,' said the victim. Justice prevailed, and Bhura was awarded life imprisonment. What society do we live in where a rapist thinks it is the woman who is stigmatised and he is not?

Why do some rape victims accept marriage to rapists? Dr Manjeet Bhatia of Women's Studies and Development Centre, Delhi University, thinks this is an extension of social attitudes towards the crime. 'The internalisation of being stigmatised for life is so deeply ingrained in the victim that she actually believes that marrying her rapist is the only way out,' Bhatia says. And so the practice continues.

Dr Rajat Mitra, psychologist and director, Swarnchetan, an NGO that counsels victims of such crimes, says it cautions rape victims against marrying their attackers, telling them that such marriages are disastrous and are marked by further violence. But not every victim is willing to heed this advice. 'When we tell people, for example, her family members, that she cannot live with somebody who has caused her such trauma, they brush it aside saying that the girl would get over it,' says Mitra.

Rape is one of the many manifestations of violence against

women placed in a much wider continuum of socially and politically inflicted violence. Society has castrated women in every which way. Rape is just one dimension of this castration. It is a means by which she is politically manipulated to nourish feelings of guilt, fear, distrust, anger and frustration. The law, ironically, chooses to harass and distrust the victim rather than give her justice. In all rulings on rape cases, people conveniently forget that rape bears a direct relation to power structures in a given society. This relationship is not a simple, mechanical one but involves complex structures reflecting the interconnectedness of gender, caste and class oppression that characterises society.

If we refuse to understand the nature of sexual violence as is mediated by caste, class, race and state power, we have no hope of developing strategies that will allow us to purge society of oppressive, misogynist violence. We do not realise that to grasp the true nature of sexual assault, we must place it within its larger political context. If we wish to understand the true nature of rape as experienced by women as individuals, we must be aware of its social mediations. The high incidence of casteist rape, incestuous rape, marital rape and communal rape in India against the backdrop of a corrupt and tottering democracy, heightening poverty and ethnic terrorism, equals the rape of women in Nicaragua against its backdrop of imperialist violence, against the backdrop of apartheid in South Africa, the racist-inspired violence on Afro-Americans and other racially oppressed people in the United States.

Rape cannot be separated from the larger spectrum of violence against women that could range from 'simple' harassment to murder. It is just another weapon in the arsenal that keeps patriarchy alive and thriving. It is the attitude of misogyny central to institutional structures that is responsible for maintaining individual violence, including rape. This misogyny results in the blaming and the shaming of the victim, two accepted modes of treatment in the South Asian community. We must recognise that such treatments creates and sustains a deadly conspiracy of silence around the whole issue of rape. It punishes the victim and causes her to bear the burden of violation in isolation and allows the perpetrator undeserved freedom.

Political leaders who offer humiliating solutions to grave problems, leaders who surrender to acceptable responses defined by a patriarchal culture can never understand the extent of female oppression and the tenacity of patriarchy. Nor can they offer real solutions to complex social, historical and political problems arising out of the very gender-bias patriarchy thrives on. Can monetary compensation restore the lost dignity and self-esteem of the victim? Think about it.

Family Planning And Gender Bias

AGAINST THE BACKDROP of the sterilizing deaths in Chhattisgarh in 2014, where fifteen women lost their lives after tubectomies conducted under horrific conditions, it would be in context to look back and find that this has been happening for decades. Ever since family planning strategies began focussing on women as targets of the government's population stabilisation programmes with little or no regard to the quality of lives of the people targeted.

India is the first country in the world to have introduced family planning as a national programme. It is also the first country that coined the phrase 'Family Planning' to replace the earlier term 'birth control.' The word 'welfare' was incorporated in 1977 and we had the new term 'Family Welfare Planning.' The word 'welfare' was meant to introduce quality-oriented programmes because till then, all family planning strategies were targeted at quantity.

The question here is quality for whom and at what cost? Did they mean the quality of the future population? Or did this suggest a rise in the quality of the standard of living for the poorest of the poor who continue to live without any 'standard' at all?

Rural health activist Manisha Gupte in her unpublished paper *A Feminist Understanding of Contraception* (1986) writes: 'Few topics related to the women's health movement are as controversial as contraception. Liberating heterosexual women, at one end, by giving them the choice to control their own reproduction, on the other end snatches away the same control when many contraceptives that are abrasive and harmful come as a package deal with population control programmes that select, motivate and wherever necessary, coerce helpless targets. Male hegemony exists in medicine, in policy, in decision-making and in research. Do women end up having lesser choice and lesser control over their bodies through the usage of existing contraceptives?'

The answers to these questions are relevant nearly three decades after Gupte raised them. Sterilisations performed in 2013-14 exceeded four million, according to the government. India had the world's third-highest female sterilisation rate after the Dominican Republic and Puerto Rico among more than 180 countries tracked by the United Nations. Fourteen women died post-sterilisation surgery in a camp in Chhattisgarh where 83 surgeries were performed in six hours. On the same day, another woman, belonging to the primate tribe protected by law, died from another sterilisation camp in the same state though the government has banned the sterilisation of women of this endangered tribe.

Methods of Contraception
The Oral Pill

A close look at different devices adopted to push Family Planning in India reveal that almost all programmes are tilted against women. Other than the male sterilisation scandal created by the then ruling party in 1977, every single technology in the programme has been targeted at women. Rural, poor and uneducated women have often been willing and often ignorant participants in the process, submitting themselves unwittingly as guinea pigs to a larger aim that sacrifices them to a cause that is as self-defeating in its means as it is destructive in its ends.

Most of the oral pills used as a contraceptive device by women are Schedule L drugs. Yet, they were advertised on television, though such drugs are prohibited from being advertised. Besides, no woman who opts for the oral pill adheres to WHO directives such as:

(a) compulsory supervision by a medical expert
(b) the woman must go through a thorough screening of her system to rule out contra-indications
(c) while on the pill, she must undergo periodic check-ups so that negative side-effects, if any, may be detected and the woman be asked to stop the pill
(d) she must be educated about the importance of taking the pill everyday
(e) she must be made aware of the side effects that could ensue from continuous use of the pill
(f) she must know what she should do if she has forgotten to take the pill

To add to this, in 2006, the government permitted the ECP (Emergency Contraceptive Pill) to be used as a convenient form of contraception in case the woman or the girl has forgotten to take protection during sex. This is freely advertised across television screens in the country. Though young urban girls look at it as their freedom to choose 'the morning after' pill denied to them for so long. 'Girls are popping these pills like candies,' says Dr Abhijit Ghosh, a gynecologist at Kolkata's Bhagirathi Neotia Women and Child Care Centre. 'They are not aware that multiple use of the pill in a menstrual cycle can lead to contraception failure which is quite difficult to diagnose. Frequent use can affect fertility in the long run,' he says.

The effects of long-term overuse, according to doctors, are still being studied. Besides, there are common side-effects like nausea, vomiting, headache, abdominal bleeding, irregular menstrual cycles.

IUDs

Intra-Uterine Devices (IUDs) were prescribed as a temporary fertility control measure developed by Dr Jack Lippes, who came to India to introduce and counsel on this method. In 1981, the Indian Council of Medical Research claimed that IUDs are effective, reversible and economical. But possible complications are perforation of the uterus, pelvic inflammatory disease, spontaneous abortions and increasing chances of ectopic pregnancy. A US Food and Drug Administration panel recommended that both physicians and IUD users should be made thoroughly aware of the increased risk of inflammatory disease and possible interference with future infertility. In January 1986, both Copper-7 and Tatum T, two IUDs manufactured by GD Searle were withdrawn from the US market but their marketing overseas did not stop. Note that these devices were exclusively for women.

A notorious IUD marketed by US multinational AH Robins was the Dalkon Shield. The company marketed approximately 1.7 million of the device to at least 80 countries. Its inventor Dr Hugh J Davis of John Hopkins Medical School in Baltimore claimed that the pregnancy rate with its use was only 1.1 per cent. It did not need FDA clearance because it was not a drug. Women who got the IUD inserted began to complain of serious discomfort like:

- pelvic inflammatory disease
- sterility
- spontaneous abortions,
- loss of reproductive organs; 200,000 deaths were reported in the US alone. These facts were kept hidden by AH Robins and distribution continued. In 1974, the FDA stopped distribution until its safety was ascertained. Finally, the Dalkon Shield was recalled but the damage was done, especially in Third World countries like India where women were not able to identify the brand and type of IUD they were using. They had no prescription at hand to trace it back to the company.

The Sixth Five Year Plan that introduced IUD, oral pills and sterilisation as methods of contraception and Family Planning earned notoriety through what came to be known as the 'Great Copper-T Fraud' in Maharashtra. In 1983, public health officials operating in Sindhudurg and Thane districts were hell-bent on bagging the coveted Rs 2.5 crore first prize for the third year in succession initiated by the government.

Investigations revealed a massive scam of manufactured

statistics of people who were acceptors of Copper-T insertions while in reality, the insertions had not taken place at all. The Copper-Ts scheduled to be inserted were misappropriated and to bag the prize, the public health officials claimed a 256 per cent success over the targeted figure!

Abortion

The Medical Termination of Pregnancy (MTP) Act of 1971 was patterned after the British Abortion Act of 1967. Abortion in India, however, was legalised not as a weapon to bring down the birth rate unlike most countries but (i) on broad grounds, (ii) on eugenic considerations, (iii) under judicial conditions such as rape or incest and (iv) socially relevant reasons such as mental or social injury to the pregnant woman. However, experience and statistics have shown that inspite of legalisation of abortion, illegal abortions are rampant. The Health Ministry on the basis of the Shah Committee Report stated that between April 1972 and March 1983, of a total of 42.9 million abortions, only 3.11 million abortions were registered under the law while the rest, it is presumed, were illegal and led to a large number of deaths.

In other words, the MTP Act did not help bring down the hazards of induced abortions because for lack of counselling and proper publicity, many women remained unaware of abortion having been legalised and went to quacks for a quick abortion much beyond the safe period.

The late Dr Malini Karkal of the International Institute of Population Studies, rightly said, 'Those who advocate termination of pregnancy on grounds that the woman should be given the right to decide about herself do not realise that giving rights without provision of powers to implement the rights become an added instrument of exploitation.'

Sterilisation

With the declaration of Emergency in 1976, a national target of 4.3 million sterilisations was announced by the government earmarked for the period between April 1976 and March 1977. The brunt of these male vasectomies was borne by poor, illiterate, ignorant, low-caste and minority men involving coercion at the highest level. Several teenaged boys were also forced to undergo vasectomy. This scandal was partly the reason for the then ruling party's downfall in the following elections. The next government, therefore, and others thereafter, have deliberately and calculatedly reduced male vasectomy programmes over the past decades. There has been a visible shift bringing the burden almost totally on women. Then Health Minister Mohsina Kidwai admitted in 1986 that over the past years, vasectomy cases had declined sharply.

The death chronicles began when in 1985, forty-four women in Rajasthan died on the operation table while undergoing sterilisation for want of post-operative care. A few like Gita Rawal and Suman Sethia suffered a state worse than death. After a tubectomy on 1 August 1985, Suman went into coma for three months. When she regained consciousness, she was paralysed from the waist down. Gita turned into a joke of the woman she once was. She went for a sterilisation operation on 7 July 1987 and had to be confined in bed to prevent her limbs from getting completely gnarled. Gita Rawal was tempted with the offer of a soft loan for a sewing machine in exchange for undergoing the operation.

Swapna Majumdar in an article in The Women's Feature Service reports 'About 2,700 cases of failure, complication or death due to sterilisation were officially recorded in 2012. According to the Ministry of Health and Family Welfare, while Rajasthan recorded the highest number of failures in sterilisation cases at 772, Tamil Nadu accounted for the maximum number of deaths at 10, followed by Andhra Pradesh and Madhya Pradesh at eight deaths each, Bihar, Karnataka and Rajasthan at four deaths each and Assam, Gujarat and Uttar Pradesh at two deaths each. Forty per cent of the 225 million women sterilised worldwide live in India. More than half the women who get sterilised have had the operation before they reach 26 years of age.'

Other Methods

Other methods of long-term hormonal contraceptives such as Dep Provera which was banned by the US but continued to be exported through manufacture by Upjohn Pharmaceuticals' Belgian agencies outside US to countries like India. Thankfully, after the storm it created in the UK and the US, the Indian government decided not to allow its use and distribution in India. NET_EN is another long-term hormonal contraceptive whose implementation and use fizzled out after women and health activists questioned the use of clinical trials of NET-EN conducted by the Indian Council of Medical Research where WHO rules of experiments are violated with impunity. Needless to say, men do not feature in any of these methods. Has medical research and research in medical technology forgotten that men exist and also need to participate in controlling the size of their respective families?

Motivators and Health Workers

In India, motivators are also poor women who have to reach target results. 'Though in principle, the government has adapted a target-free approach in 1995, targets continue to haunt the service providers. Government camps are organised to achieve the targets. It is imminent that India's promise at the July 2012 Family Planning 2020 Summit to increase access to 200 million couples and adolescents will reinforce the pressures of targets furthermore in coming years,' says Dr AL Sharada, Director, Population First, NGO based in Mumbai that works for the girl child.

In the mid-eighties, the government decided to disband male community health volunteers in the Family Planning project because it was increasingly felt that in the Indian social climate, rural women rejected male volunteers and health workers. Has the induction of women helped in any way? Not if one takes cognisance of incidents of botched sterilisation operations, rat-poison in anesthesia and two minutes for each surgery. To fulfill the targets, one must remember that motivators are also women from very poor backgrounds. In a hurry to fulfill targets, they motivate as many women as they can to attend each sterilisation camp. Initially, it was a precondition that women health workers or motivators must first become acceptors themselves so that their methods of persuasion are backed by experience. But was this practice monitored and supervised?

The use of women instead of men makes coercion easy, quick and convenient. Says Gupte, 'When motivators are women, be they health staff or primary school teachers, they are constantly threatened with dire consequences such as job transfer, sexual harassment, humiliation and delayed money if they fail to fulfill their targets.' In March 1986, Manda Padwal, a female health worker in Talaseri Primary Health Centre in Thane, Maharashtra, committed suicide after being reprimanded by the doctor-in-charge for not fulfilling the specified target of sterilising 20 tribals in the area.

In *Choice and Coercion – Birth Control, Sterlization and Abortion is Public Health and Welfare*, Johanna Schoen, the author's statement emphasises how universal this strategy is. She states that in August 2003, North Carolina became the first US state to offer restitution to victims of state-ordered sterilisations carried out by its eugenics programme between 1929 and 1975. The decision was prompted, she adds, largely by a series of articles in *The Winston-Salem Journal*. These stories were inspired in part by the author's research who was granted unique access to summaries of 7,500 case histories and papers of the North Carolina Eugenics Board. Schoen widens her focus to include birth control, sterilisation and abortion policies across the nation and demonstrates how each method of limiting unwanted pregnancies had the potential, both to expand and to limit the women's productive choices. Such programmes overwhelmingly targeted poor and non-white population yet they also extended a measure of reproductive control to poor women.

To sum up, this writer would like to quote from health journalist Vimal Balasubramiam's article 'Towards a Woman's Perspective on Family Planning' in *The Economic and Political Weekly*: 'The paradox which characterises the family planning scene in India is this—on the one hand, women are the major targets of the FP programme with both messages and methods beamed intensively at them; on the other hand, the felt contraception needs of these women who predominantly belong to the lower socio-economic class, are not adequately catered to. In a country like India, women can be doubly victimised: by the patriarchal family which refuses to allow them to use contraception and by the population controllers who make them the targets of unsafe contraceptive programmes.'

Should Men Take Responsibility to Stop Violence Against Women?

SHOULD MEN TAKE responsibility to stop violence against women? To mark the beginning of the International Campaign to Stop Violence Against Women and Girls, Swayam, a city-based NGO, stressed on this specific question. The purpose is to create public awareness on the issue of violence against women and girls, draw more men into the struggle to gain and establish the rights of women and girls, break the conspiracy of silence that surrounds all kinds of violence against women and girls, and incorporate men in these programmes of awareness, consciousness-raising and action to bring these issues out in the open.

It is both interesting and ironical to find that in a patriarchal society, men are accused of sustaining a feudal, sometimes even fascist approach towards women and are perpetrators of violence on women directly and indirectly, covertly and overtly, in physical, emotional, financial and legal terms. According to the National Crime Records Bureau (Ministry of Home Affairs), 2006, every day, six women committed suicide linked to dowry, 23 women were killed for the same reason, 53 were raped and 128 women were sexually harassed.

Across India, there is a long list of social reformers who undertook major efforts for bringing about revolutionary changes in the status and position of women. In Bengal, Iswar Chandra Vidyasagar championed female education and led the campaign to legalise widow remarriage. Keshub Chandra Sen, a leader of the Brahmo Samaj, tried to invest women with new roles through schools, prayer meetings and experiments in living. By the turn of the century, Swami Vivekananda, leader of an activist order of Hindu monasticism, argued that women could become a powerful regenerative force. In North India, Swami Dayananda Saraswati, founder of the Arya Samaj, encouraged female education and condemned customs he regarded as derogatory to women such as marriage between partners of unequal ages, dowry and polygyny. Rai Salig Ram, also known as Huzur Maharaj, a follower of the Radhasoami faith, advocated female emancipation in *Prem Patra*, his prose volumes.

Among Muslims, Khwaja Altaf Husain Ali and Shaikh Muhammad Abdullah introduced education for girls. In Western India, Mahadev Govind Ranade founded the National Social Conference to focus attention on social reforms. Journalist Behramji Malabari captured the attention of the British reading public with his articles in *The Times* (London) on the evils of child marriage and the tragedy of enforced widowhood for young women. Dhondo Keshav Karve offered a practical solution in Pune, setting up institutions to educate young widows so that they could teach in girls' schools. In South

India, R Venkata Ratnam Naidu opposed the *Devadasi* system while Virasalingam Pantulu worked towards the reformation in the institution of marriage. Both of them worked towards opportunities for female education.

'Men like Ram Mohan Roy and Iswar Chandra Vidyasagar tried to redraw the traditional definition of woman and identity, trying to introduce into it new elements drawn from reinterpreted tradition,' writes Ashis Nandy. The ideas in the minds of most nineteenth century male reformers lie in the fact that these were rooted in their personal experience. During their lifetime, they attempted to change those with whom they lived and worked. It was not as if they were responding and reacting to British pressure.

A little-known fact about scriptural sanctions of *sati* comes to light when Lata Mani traces the widespread anti-*sati* campaigns of Raja Rammohan Roy (1772-1833.) 'Roy drew upon the *Bhagwad Gita*, among other texts, in presenting his case against the practice to his co-religionists. The basic argument he used in support of the abolition of *sati* was the doctrine of desireless action or *nishkama karma* as propounded in the *Gita*. His argument was that the goal of heaven sought by the act of *sati* was an end inferior to that of salvation, to which women were fully entitled. According to the *Bhagwad Gita*, an ascetic way of life spent in desireless work was the only way to attain salvation. This fact is unknown to many because scholars of Hindu scriptures believe that the *Bhagwad Gita* became prominent within Hinduism only in the latter part of the nineteenth century.

'Debates on women, whether in the context of *sati*, widow remarriage or *zenanas* (seclusion of women) were not merely about women, but also instances in which the moral challenge of colonial rule was confronted and negotiated. In this process women came to represent "tradition" for all participants: whether viewed as the weak, deluded creatures who must be reformed through legislation and education, or the valiant keepers of tradition who must be protected from the first and be permitted only certain kinds of instruction.

'For the British, rescuing women becomes part of the civilising mission. For the indigenous elite, protection of their status or their reform becomes an urgent necessity, in terms of the honour of the collective—religious or national. For all participants of the nineteenth century debates on social reform, women represent embarrassment or potential. And given the discursive construction of women as either abject victims or heroines, they frequently represent both shame and promise.'

However, historian Sumit Sarkar has voiced a point of dissent. He argues that these reformers were concerned primarily with modifying relationships within their own families and sought only 'limited and controlled emancipation of their womenfolk.' His argument is based on the premise that women themselves were not partners in these programmes for their change and upliftment. They were often portrayed as opposed to their own liberation. Without first-hand accounts from these women, their reluctance to change in the ways prescribed by their husbands and fathers could be read as nascent feminist resistance, an intelligent reading of their true interests, or plain and simple opposition to any change.

Ageing
A Positive Approach

AGEING, AT FIRST glance, does not appear to discriminate on grounds of gender. But a closer look reveals cracks that might not apply, to the same degree, to old men. Men might not be as vulnerable to distress and misery in old age to the same extent as women. The main reason is that women in India form a small percentage of the working population. Thus, they are denied the retirement benefits that working men have access to when they retire from work.

An interesting finding emerged in the results of a survey conducted by the Calcutta Metropolitan Institute of Gerontology, started in 1988, through a questionnaire distributed among men and women about to retire. While 61.23 per cent of the male respondents spoke of economic problems as a major off-shoot of retirement, a significant percentage of 40.9 among the females claimed that they did not anticipate any problems at all. This sounds ironical in a social environment where old women are constantly being edged out of their own homes and their children's homes when they lose their husbands.

Patriarchy has seen to it that a major share of movable and immovable assets within an extended Indian family, including financial documents and land, are managed and controlled by the men in the family. They are held in the names of the women—wives and daughters-in-law, true, but purely for tax purposes. These women have no control over these assets even after the male head of the family passes away or becomes senile. The control automatically passes over to the son or sons and the old woman is left in the lurch, financially speaking. In nuclear families, the mother or unmarried older sister has to live with grown-up children or brothers and sisters who have their own families. While some children, who lead working lives, might look upon an ageing mother as a blessing in disguise/unpaid babysitter/nurse/cook—all rolled in one, this is more an exception than the rule.

There are outstanding women who are as active as women half their age despite having crossed sixty. 'Ageing does not mean slowing down. In celebration of this fact, *Harmony* for Silvers Foundation proudly honoured 10 Silver achievers for their contributions towards the well being of the society,' Foundation chairperson Tina Ambani said when the awards were launched in 2007.

Indian women form a significant majority of the elderly population in India. Estimates state that there are 99 men to every 100 women belonging to the age-group 60-64 years in developing countries. In the age-group of 80+, the male-female ratio tilts against the males with 69 males to every 100 women.

The position of single women is more precarious because few are willing to take care of non-linear relatives. A majority of widows have no independent source of income and the worst nightmare for them is old age. PN Mari Bhat of the Population Research Centre in Darwad concludes from his study on 'Widows and Widowhood Mortality in India' that widows have a higher mortality rate than women whose husbands are alive. Around 50 per cent of widows in India are under the age of 60.

The belief that widows are taken care of by their parental families is a myth, especially in rural India where less than six per cent live with their in-laws or parents while 10 per cent live with their married daughters. Around 60 per cent get regular support from their sons, 16 per cent are cared for by daughters, 9 per cent by brothers, 5 per cent by parents and 3 per cent by in-laws. No study on widowhood gives an account of the castaway widows of Varanasi and Vrindaban who are totally shunned, their families having left them to die. Pensions for widows are limited and arbitrary. The eligibility and amounts differ from state to state with Kerala forking out a meagre Rs 70 a month regardless of the widow's other sources of income, class, age or whether she has an adult son. The Karnataka government raised widow pension from Rs 50 to Rs 75 a month in 1994.

In India, women with sons alone can rely on domestic support from them in old age. But changing behaviour patterns among the young, resulting from pressures of inflation, shortage of housing space in urban metros, the steadily increasing stress on consumerism, the declining importance given to emotions and sentiments and the rising costs of raising children have all but wiped out the possible support aged women could expect their sons to give them. In terms of healthcare services too, old women are placed on the wrong end of the welfare axis because the entire focus is on family planning, and mother-and-child care. Old women find no place in policy decisions covering the health of women.

In this negative environment, it came as a pleasant surprise when a United Nations Expert Group Meeting on Integration of Ageing and Elderly Women into Development held in 1991 took constructive and positive steps towards harnessing the productive capabilities of older women so that they can create and sustain a financially independent future and that their productivity can be used for the betterment of the nation in general and the institution of the family in particular. The meeting recognised that major efforts had to be made to ensure the access of elderly women to basic education and information on the ageing process, learning skills—both traditional and non-traditional, and retraining as and when called for.

Besides formal education, Participatory Rural Approval (PRA) provides ways to learn with and from older people, especially women since it has been observed that women have a perspective that is completely different from men and this perspective can make a greater impact on the economic and social lives of these communities. The PRA experiment combines a number of approaches so that a community can conduct its own analysis and planning and share its experience with professionals. It is here that older women can be more helpful and creatively productive than older men.

Older women have the potential to make valuable contributions to society reaching beyond the limited and rigid framework of their immediate families. They constantly persevere to put their experience gained from life to productive use for social benefit. For example, older women are often called upon to attend to the sick and the dying. They also hand down their traditional modes of learning and experience to the next generation such as grandmother's medicines, pre and post-natal healthcare for mother and infant, household hygiene, diet and nutrition. Such services go unrecognised and unpaid because they cannot be quantified in economic terms. Old women play a vital role in transmitting the accumulated wisdom and knowledge they have gained over their lifetime to the generations of the present and the future. They also contribute significantly to the maintenance of traditions and values that need to be upheld for sustaining our cultural roots.

The world offers ample examples of elderly women who are still actively taking part in rebuilding the lives of refugees traumatised by disaster or war. The political participation of elderly women in world politics is now a part of living history. Many elderly women have been elected as the administrative and executive heads of their respective states. Supposedly on the margins, they continue to cook and care and nurse and clean and take care of the family marketing and budgeting long after they have crossed sixty. Grandmothers are known to be the best educators of their grandchildren, handing down to them tales of mythology and history, of wisdom and fables no longer taught in formal educational institutions. Yet these contributions are completely ignored when the same women need to fall back on some kind of emotional support from the very families they nurtured through their lives.

Ageing, especially among women, is still sadly taken to

be a purely biological inevitability. Most women still consider menopause as the end of the world. What we seem to forget is that age is a cultural category. Its meaning and significance vary both historically and cross-culturally. It is time we began to challenge the stereotyping of ageing women as an assumed homogeneity. Class, race, gender and culture can counter biological factors. Thankfully, there is growing research interest in this field, not only in the experience and ethnography of the aged, but also in the specific constructions of 'old age' across cultures and through time, with special attention being paid to elderly women.

Journey Of A Woman Priestess

IN THE HISTORY of Indian cinema, no director has explored the story of a woman priest. Women have been barred from this profession because they are considered 'impure' to perform religious rituals and rites during pujas, weddings, funerals and thread ceremonies.

Why? The reason that is usually given is that since women menstruate for three or four days every month, they cannot perform rituals and religious ceremonies. The second is that women get pregnant and how can pregnant women be permitted to perform pujas on a regular basis? The third reason is that all *mantras* need to be pronounced in an order of increasing and decreasing voice (*swara*) that sometimes demands the holding of breath to complete a mantra precisely and accurately, failing which, the rituals and the poojas may not be pure and perfect. This holding of breath puts pressure on the—the *garbha*(uterus) which may create trouble later on for young women of fertile age. The fourth is that Brahmin women do not have the 'thread' ceremony that is a sanctioned ritual to declare a person as being a 'Brahmin.'

However, these 'rules' that proscribe women from stepping into sacred chambers to perform prayers are dictated by rigid patriarchal norms in general and religious heads of the Hindus, temple priests and Brahmins of a high order in particular. Besides, the physical taboos do not stand the test of logic because menstruation and pregnancy are a biological reality for every female that cannot be changed and that cannot be used as an excuse to keep women away from priesthood as bestowing them with priesthood may shake the very foundations of patriarchal rule and patriarchal control over the religious pantheon in Hinduism.

In fact, times have changed. Pune has a special school to train women as priests which has around 200 students studying the Vedas, Sanskrit mantras and detailed rituals for every Hindu ceremony. They learn to recite ancient Sanskrit scriptures—a skill that is helping them challenge male supremacy in conducting religious ceremonies. Varanasi too began a school on similar vein. At the Pune-based Udyan Mangal Karyalaya (meaning 'The Garden of Good'), women are given formal training in priesthood. Here they study the Hindu philosophical texts in Sanskrit and learn to recite them.

Panini Kanya Mahavidyalaya Gurukul in Varanasi also has a training scheme for girls to be ordained into priesthood. They not only learn to recite the Gayatri Mantra which girls were not allowed to learn or chant but are also trained in traditional martial arts besides learning the Vedas and from other Hindu scriptures. Those who have graduated perform weddings, naming ceremonies, thread ceremonies, *annaprashanas*, death rites and funeral rites. It is run by the Arya Samaj. As they are trained in music, they sing in chorus which adds a new dimension to every ceremony they conduct. They work in singles and in groups while there is one priestess who conducts the main rituals. They also have another school in Mumbai at Kakadwadi and Acharya Nandita Shastri heads the school as a principal.

V.L. Manjul, research scholar and chief librarian at Pune's Bhandarkar Oriental Research Institute, estimates that India now has around 1,600 of women priests. In Maharashtra alone, 'Some 600 women have been trained as *purohits*' (priests), he says. Pune-based Shankar Seva Samiti and Jnana Prabhodini are two leading schools that sixteen years ago formally began to train women to conduct rituals, prayers for initiation, engagement, marriage, conversion, house warming, ancestor worship and last rites. Women here undergo the grind of studying Sanskrit, learning by heart all the verses from ancient texts that are necessary to conduct ceremonies.

The issue of women priests made headlines in August 2014 after a 900-year-old temple in Maharashtra's pilgrimage city of Pandharpur appointed one, breaking its centuries-old tradition of a male Brahmin priest leading ceremonies. Local Brahmin families claimed ancestral rights over the temple but in January, the Supreme Court stripped their right to appoint priests and collect and keep donations. The state government then set up a managing committee, which interviewed 129 candidates from all castes before appointing a woman.

Arya Joshi is a teacher in a priesthood course in Pune and a Sanskrit researcher herself. She did her doctorate on ancestral

Hindu worship. In an interview, she pointed out that Hinduism had never barred women from performing religious rites. There is even mention of them in ancient religious writings. Later, when men came to dominate the profession, they declared that priests could only be male and only from a particular Hindu caste. That thinking prevails till today.

'The problem occurs because I think people do not have an exact idea of women priesthood', Joshi added. 'They don't know that this is an ancient tradition for the past 5,000 years. It is a typical orthodox mindset. Some 25 per cent of the people are not ready to accept women priesthood. But we think it will change with time, so we have to wait for that.'

Megha Gokhale, a woman priest living in Navi Mumbai's Belapur township, says the impact of education and urbanisation has spurred feminism, ushering significant changes in religious practices of Indian women, affecting their religious status too. She conducts classes near her home for some 50 students, both girls and boys, teaching them the nuances of conducting rituals, ceremonies and performing religious incantations. 'Women are the torch bearers of religion and play a pivotal role in preserving religion and culture,' she says.

When women are breaking male bastions in every field from driving train engines to running a truck service and serving in petrol stations, there is no reason they should be kept away from becoming priests.

Is The Prostitute Not A 'Worker'?

WHEN SEXUAL PLEASURE is a marketable service, how can the person who sells this service be excluded from the category of 'workers' to be bracketed as a 'non-worker' along with the beggar and the prisoner?

The Census of India lists homemakers, beggars, prisoners and prostitutes as 'non-workers' because they are 'economically non-productive workers' by perception and definition by the Census. The 'homemaker' being a non-worker has already been dealt with by the Supreme Court last year. But the prostitute remains beyond the 'working' framework. Why? Does the prostitute not earn money? Does she not sell the service of her body for a price to her clients on a time-work basis?

When NGOs and social activists pressed the Establishment to change the term of the trader from 'prostitute' to sex-worker, this was accepted in usage but not in legal or official terms. But the 'worker' added to 'sex' automatically implies that money is exchanged for services rendered. So how can the Census consider the sex worker to be a non-productive consumer?

How can the apex court that passed a ruling stating that the housewife is a 'worker' missed out on the anomaly in the case of the prostitute? Is it because the prostitute belongs to a marginalised section of society like the beggar and the prisoner? Or, is it because she is more concerned about the social stigma her occupation burdens her with along with the constant threat of unprotected sex than about her inclusion in the Census as a 'worker' who contributes to the country's GNP? Or, maybe it is because her 'work' is considered 'illegal' and as such, does not fall within the eligibility rules of Census calculations?

Indian law statutes define prostitution as the act of a female who offers her body for promiscuous sexual intercourse for hire, in exchange for money or kind. The two conditions that defines a woman to be a prostitute according to the Suppression of Immoral Traffic in Women and Girls Act, 1956 (amended in 1987 by the Amendment Act 1986 with the name changed to read Immoral Traffic (Prevention) Act and the 2006 Bill are:

(a) a female has to offer her body for indiscriminate sexual intercourse

(b) she should do so for some financial consideration. This is the legal definition. It spells out that she is a productive worker because her work has both use-value and exchange-value

The 'illicitness' of commercial sex is due to social disapproval. When women place monetary value and claim payment for work that they traditionally (within marriage) perform for 'free'—out of love, instinct, for intangible non-monetary rewards, it is viewed as 'betrayal.' At the same time, when professions get 'feminized' in the wage market such as prostitution, almost a totally feminized occupation, they get devalued. Perceived from this angle, commercial sex is nothing more than an inferior version of 'real' or free and romantic sex.

Slippages between women who are prostitutes and sell sex for money, and women who are not considered prostitutes as sex is structured into a married relationship are many in theory, argument and practice. Examples that blur the distinctions between the two are the contractual terms of bourgeois marriage, women's confessions to 'occasional prostitution', sex for favours, sex inscribed into certain professions, describing women who are promiscuous as whores and so on. Luce Irigary states that the prostitute's 'value' cannot be categorised either as use-value or as exchange-value (the mother and the virgin respectively representing the female 'types' of these values). She adds that prostitution amounts to usage that is exchanged. Irigary insists that she is only an object of exchange between and among men, the pimp and the client. Shannon Bell in *Reading, Writing and Re-Writing the Prostitute Body*, 1994, writes that the ambiguous unity in the prostitute body of use and exchange value positions her as a speaking subject which makes her 'an active participant who exchanges her own use-value.'

Catherine Cowley, in a study conducted under IHHR/FFDA, tacitly points out how 'the supply of women from lower castes into the sex trade is driven by the demand for prostitutes, though prostitution is illegal in India. Its very existence and pervasiveness in Indian society is an anomaly in an otherwise conservative country. Yet, there is a historic culture of commercial sex in India, with eroticism enshrined in the myriad religious traditions. Consequently, there is greater tolerance of prostitution in areas, usually rural, where it is seen as a continuation of a cultural tradition.' The study focusses on young girls among the Bedni tribe in Madhya Pradesh where Raveena, 18, became a prostitute to support her family. She is the sole breadwinner of an extended family of 20. There is 'tremendous pressure to provide for my family in the only way I know how.' Where will you place this girl from the Bedni tribe?

Categorised by the Constitution of India as Scheduled Caste, the Bedni caste has traditionally been relegated to the most menial labour, discriminated against and excluded by the wider community, with no possibility of upward mobility. The exertion of power by the upper castes over these lower caste prostitutes also reinforces caste hierarchy as the women's bodies represent the community.

The problem is not confined to Madhya Pradesh. Many women from lower castes, such as the Kanjar (Gujarat), Kolathi (Maharashtra) and Dewar (Chhattisgarh), are known to enter into the sex trade on the basis of their caste. If Raveena is selling her services to support a dependent family, is she not a productive worker who is creating surplus value which means, she is 'producing' more than she consumes?

Under capitalism, according to Marx, the exchange value of commodities is their inherent monetary property and that in turn, money achieves a social existence quite apart from all commodities and their natural mode of existence. The circulation of money and its abstraction as a sign in a system of exchange serves as a mirror image for women as sign in a system of exchange. Ironically, the women who form the very commodity that is exchanged have little or no control over the money that is exchanged. This is confiscated and appropriated by the ancillary trades attached to prostitution such as the brothel owner, the pimp, the bouncers, the brothel madam, the hooch seller and so on. They do not have access to the circulation of money either.

The very fact that the prostitute's value-in-exchange helps support the procurer, the pimp, the brothel owner, the brothel madam and the bouncer proves that she is a productive worker. Remove the prostitute from this infra-structure and the system will collapse. That money does not come to her or remains with her cannot deny her claim to being an economic worker whose service brings money. In a country where 'legal workers' like shameless ministers and corrupt MPs are forever involved in illegal scams, is it not a joke to consider prostitution illegal and non-productive?

THE WORLD

Women And Parliament

THE DEBATE ON the participation of women in the political process beginning from popular grassroots movements has raised several questions about awareness, impact, leadership, priorities, and so on. It has also led to many analyses on the nature of a political struggle, on mechanisms of mobilisation, strategies and perspectives on micro issues in relation to larger political processes and ideological dimensions.

Some scholars have argued that political participation of women depends largely on the historical tradition of women's participation in political and social movements and on the political milieu. To understand the political behaviour of women and the constraints of their participation, it is important to define the concepts of political status and political participation. 'Political participation' is understood generally as the voluntary participation in political affairs through the act of voting, membership and other activities related with political parties, legislative assemblies and socio-political movements. 'Political status' has been defined by the Committee on the Status of Women in India as 'the degree and equality of freedom displayed by women in the shaping and sharing of power and in the value given to women's role in the society.'

Indian women have been contesting elections from the pre-Independence era. Annie Besant, who accelerated the process of women's association in 1914 with her entry into Indian politics, was the first woman to be elected as president of the Indian National Congress. Sarojini Naidu too became active in Indian National Movement. In the 1930s, the powerful motivations of Jawaharlal Nehru made Uttar Pradesh a showcase province for women's active participation in politics. The Legislative Council and the Legislative Assembly had 16 women members. The most prominent among them were Begum Aizaz Rasul, the deputy speaker of the Legislative Council, and Vijayalakshmi Pandit, who held a cabinet post. But one must note that both these women came from highly politicised, elite families who had no first-hand knowledge of the political situation and were not in touch with the masses. After the first general elections in 1937, almost every province had a sprinkling of women legislators.

Every election from 1967 to 1984 in the post-Independence era was dominated by the towering personality of Indira Gandhi. Till 1984, among the twenty-eight women members of the Lok Sabha, two-thirds came from well-known political families and had no independent base of their own. Till the latest general elections held in March 1998, one finds that the family connection has now percolated down to regional politics also in quite a big way. Not all of them are elite or

Western educated, like Rabri Devi, but the filial connection is too obvious to be brushed aside.

One unique aspect of high-profile women in Indian politics is their political family background. Women not necessarily from elitist backgrounds, such as Ahilya Rangnekar, were from politically conscious families. Few women like Mrinal Gore came directly from the grassroots. Political power for most Indian women who rose to prominence in politics, such as Indira Gandhi, Shalinitai Patil, Sucheta Kripalani, Jayalalitha and Laxmi Parvathi was the direct outcome of their close relationships with politically important men. In journalese, we often call this 'widow-cracy' or 'daughter-cracy.' All these women have successfully extracted emotional mileage from these relationships. The situation has remained the same. Examples are Sonia Gandhi, Maneka Gandhi, Meera Kumar, Supriya Sule, Agatha Sangma, Shruti Chaudhary, Jyoti Mirdha... the list goes on.

A relatively recent addition is the entry of celebrities from the film, sports and cultural worlds into Parliament. They already have fame, popularity and money. So why to fight the elections? It gives them a sense of power their work fields do not permit indefinitely. It offers them a dream to pursue, the dream of participating in the developmental growth of the nation at first hand and to test their charisma among their millions of fans across the country.

Hema Malini, contesting for a Lok Sabha seat for the first time on a BJP ticket from Mathura, moved around in a white Audi with an orange umbrella and a lotus in her hand! Yet, in a recent interview, she said her complexion had completely changed because of the rallies. Do these people have the faintest idea about 'development' for the masses? Has Hema Malini returned to Mathura to take care of its 'bumpy roads' that have given her 'back pain'? Hema Malini defeated the Mathura incumbent Jayant Chaudhary (JLD) by 3,30,743 votes and was elected to the Lok Sabha.

But the underbelly of glamorous Parliamentarians was exposed when the media reported that the Maharashtra government has given a 2,000 sq m plot in Andheri's Ambivli area to the Natyavihar Kala Kendra, a trust run by the actor-dancer to build a dance school, at just Rs 70,000; market price for a similar plot in the area is around Rs 50 crore. On 2 February, the media dropped another bombshell reporting that she has been accused of destroying mangroves on a plot allotted to her in the 1990s.

Quoting an RTI reply provided by the Mumbai Suburban District Collectorate, activist Anil Galgali on Tuesday said the actress was allotted a plot measuring 1,741.89 square metres in Versova village and possession was granted on 4 April 1997. 'She had even made a payment of Rs 10 lakh, showed a bank balance of Rs 22.5 lakh in the accounts of Samta Sahkari Bank and given a project cost estimate of Rs 3.7 crore,' Galgali said. A year after the allotment, the collectorate slapped a show-cause notice on Hema Malini, asking why the allotment should not be cancelled for violating Coastal Regulatory Zone (CRZ) norms, he said.

Hema Malini sought to make a clean breast of the issue by denying allegations of any 'land-grabbing' and claimed that all rules and regulations were duly followed 'I ran from pillar to post for this. It's not been easy. The government has given it to me, I have not gone and grabbed it,' she countered on the 'land-grabbing' allegations. Following Galgali's RTI revelations, opposition parties including the Congress and the Nationalist Congress Party demanded a probe into the land allotment as well as its cancellation.

Rekha, nominated to the Rajya Sabha, records a below-average attendance of five per cent, which other MPs objected to. She was sworn in as a member of the Upper House in 2012. Her highest attendance at the winter session was a mere 10 per cent and she did not release any statement in her defence.

Elected in 2010, the Samajwadi Party member Jaya Bachchan was an exception, as the actor was seen taking her role as an MP more seriously than the other celebrities. As per MP Track by PRS Legislative Research, Jaya Bachchan had a 58 per cent attendance record from 2010 to 2013. Her attendance improved greatly in these three years. She has even spoken up for raging issues like the Delhi gang-rape of December 2012 and 26/11 terrorist attacks in Mumbai. She has also expressed strong reservations about the working of the Ministry of Women and Child Development on the floor of the House in August 2014. But whether she actually worked towards the goals is not recorded.

Smriti Irani is infamous for her high decibel voice on the floor of the House and media interviews. Irani rises on every occasion to counter every allegation made against her ambivalent comments in public space.

Maneka Sanjay Gandhi was the Union Minister for Women and Child Development in NDA. But she continues to focus on her role as a leading environmentalist, animal activist and a crusader for vegetarianism. She entered active politics in 1984. Since then she has won Parliamentary elections six times, starting with the Janata Dal and has served as minister in four governments. However, she is often criticised for her explosive comments on important issues. Responding to the Supreme Court's observation on the need for harsher punishment for child rapist, she ruled out chemical castration as a form of punishment, calling the step 'regressive' and a form of 'revenge' rather than punishment with a view to reform the offender. She was also pulled up for her proposal to record the sex of the foetus and monitor pregnancies by several civil society groups opposed to the idea who felt this would lead to terribly negative impact on the girl child in the country and to women's right to safe abortion.

Political participation of women over the past sixty-plus years suffices with one name: Indira Gandhi. To the world outside, women in India might appear to have total freedom and opportunity to participate in nation-building activities, politically speaking. But is this a true picture? For every Mrinal Gore, Maneka Gandhi, Sushma Swaraj and Smriti Irani, there are thousands of faceless, anonymous women with political aspirations who are losers in the political race even before they have arrived on the political landscape. The road to political success for women right across the world, one must admit, with their merits and demerits, is paved with thorns.

According to Anuradha Chadha's *Political Participation of Women: A Case Study in India*, 'Today, there is considerable increase in the percentage of women as voters. The participation of women as voters is almost equal to men. But the political participation (as a whole) of the women is not equal to men. They are still not able to get a share equivalent to men in organization that require decision making. Still, politics is dominated by men at every level of participation and women have not been regarded as significant part of the political arena.'

Women And Regional Journalism

JOURNALISM, FOR WOMEN journalists, is no longer confined to soft news critiquing the proliferation of beauty contests or a single case of domestic violence in the neighbourhood. Women journalists in India, both in the print as well as in the electronic media, are known for their commitment to their vocation, for their integrity in not 'selling out' to propaganda or cheap PR for a price, and for their moral courage in facing the dangers of war coverage or the coverage of a communal riot. When the Press Trust of India (PTI) recruited more women than men among their trainees a decade ago, begun with the system of entrance tests and interviews at entry point, Sujata Madhok of the Delhi Union of Journalists said, 'PTI seems to have chosen so many women because they did better in entrance tests, also because women have acquired a reputation for being more hardworking and disciplined.'

The history of women in language journalism in our

country dates back to more than a century. Interestingly, most of their writing applies to our social ethos today as much as it then did. Krishnabhabini Das, one of the first women writers in Bengal, in her article entitled *Shikshita Narir Pratibader Uttar*, (Response to a Protest from an Educated Woman) in *Sahitya*, (1891) wrote:

It is unjust to say that only men should cultivate that intelligence, that God has given both men and women. God could never have imparted such a great gift without a noble end in view.

Jnanadanandini Debi, in *Stri Shiksha* (Women's Education), an article published in the prestigious *Bharati* in 1882 (BS Asvin, 1288) offered a manifesto arguing the cause for women's education. She argued for a desegregation of the sexes, and proves how education is both the cause and the effect of this process. In *Shekele Katha* (Tales of Bygone Days) Swarnakumari Debi praised the reforms introduced by her father in the areas within the domestic sphere marked out exclusively for women. Yet, she did not forget to add that this 'women's world' did have its share of happiness and joy creating a space for nostalgia for a more 'democratic' tomorrow. Others who demonstrated similar fluency with the language and courage of their convictions were Sarala Debi, Hironmoyee Debi, Rasa Sundari Debi and so on.

Aunt Kolli from Navsari in Gujarat wrote in *StreeBodh*—a Gujarati journal known for its focus on social reforms—that it was wrong to blame women for marital strife and for the unhappiness of men. She pointed out that men visit *nautch* girls and spend entire nights drinking and being entertained by these women not in response to their wives' behaviour but due to their own inclinations for such enjoyment. The article was written in 1866. *Streebodh* (spelt *Streebodhe* in English) was the first journal for women in India published in Gujarati from January 1857 until the late 1950s. It was formed to offer suitable reading matter for Parsi and Hindu women, indirectly making it clear that families going through modernisation defined its target audience.

Sonal Shukla in her paper *Cultivating Minds—19th Century Gujarati Women's Journals*, (*Economic and Political Weekly*, October 26, 1991) states that with time, as its founder-editor Kabraji died and his daughter Shirin, followed by his daughter-in-law Putlibai, took up the editorship, *StreeBodh* changed its profile in terms of appearance, language and content. 'It reflected changes that were taking place during the nationalist struggle and the new role assigned to middle-class women within it,' writes Shukla.

Flash forward to this century. On 3 April 2002, Sonal Kellog, a woman reporter and her male colleague from a Surat-based newspaper were pounced upon by the police when they went into Gomtipur to interview women who had been attacked by the police themselves. Before she could take down their testimonies, policemen surrounded them both. When they went to the Police Commissioner to complain, they were told he had no time for them.

Barkha Dutt of Star News covered the Kargil war, reporting directly from the front in the midst of shelling and firing with the mercury dipping below minus degrees centigrade.

Like the editorial stance of *StreeBodh* in its later years, the profile of the woman journalist in India has also changed. Tavleen Singh (then correspondent with *The Sunday Telegraph*), who won the Sanksriti Award for Journalism, in one of her most memorable pieces, expressed her intense shame for being born a Sikh herself after she had met Bhindranwala and his followers at the Golden Temple.

She wrote another historic report on the murder of Sumeet Singh, editor of *Preet Lari*. Anjali Puri, then with the *Indian Express*, covered the elections in Pakistan extensively, which returned Benazir Bhutto as the first woman PM of Pakistan. Sheela Barse won the PUCL Award for her contribution to investigative journalism focusing on human rights. She trod the rather uneven and rough terrain of women prisoners in the country, going from one jail to another, crossing insurmountable hurdles on the way, going on to examine human rights violations of juvenile offenders in Hyderabad prisons, then exploring the dingy and dark world of child labourers in the machine looms of Bhiwandi, near Mumbai.

Shahnaz Anklesaria, erstwhile of *The Statesman* and then with the *Indian Express*, also won the India Today-PUCL Award for human rights in journalism for her 'devotion to a free and open society with which she laboured to secure and defend civil liberties and human rights of the disadvantaged in the country.' Shahnaz got the award for the whole body of her work in contrast to the previous winners who won the same award for individual stories. Along with the late Neerja Chowdhury (also a PUCL Awardee) Shahnaz toured Punjab soon after Operation Bluestar. She is one of the first Indian journalists to report on the local response to the government's action.

From a report by Usha Rai upon her return from the first International Women's Media conference held in Washington, DC in November 1986, we learn that the director of development at the Columbia School of Journalism states that between 1976 and 1986, 60 per cent of students at journalism schools in the US consisted of women. Yet, there remains a greater discrepancy in the salaries of men and women journalists employed in the print media than in radio or television. Nearly 90 per cent of editors responsible for women's news are women. Of the 400,000 professional journalists in China, one-third are women who write about everything from politics to science. According to Vesna Prijam, an economic writer for Yugoslavia's *Tanjug*, most successful women journalists in the country were either single or divorced.

Women's journalism has three dimensions. One concerns women actively involved in contributing the power of their voice and perspective to journalism. This is journalism *by* women. The second relates to the portrayal of women in the print media. This defines 'journalism *about* women.' Examples of this could be found in coverage of women's issues, news reports about a woman having been raped or murdered, some woman having bagged an international award, women portrayed in photo features, cartoons and comic strips, and so on. There is a specialised third dimension, which segregates the woman question through a proliferation of women's magazines across the board. This purportedly targets women and could be termed 'journalism *for* women.' This aims to retrace its steps to recall the beginnings of women journalists in India—the area spanning journalism *by* women bringing us to the present day when the gender of the journalist is completely beyond question when it comes to discussing merit, efficiency, contribution and integrity.

Women, War And Conflict Journalism

IN AN ARTICLE that traces the journey and accomplishments of women war correspondents, titled *Female War Journalists Known For Their Exceptional Courage*, Kuldeep Chauhan covers seven war correspondents in which there is just one Indian woman – Barkha Dutt. Does this mean that Indian women shy away from reporting on war and conflict zones? Or, is it that they are kept away precisely because they are women?

A closer look reveals that even among the large number of journalists reporting on war and conflict zones from English-speaking countries, Chauhan could point out only six! This is a shocking anomaly compared to men who report, write, comment and work on editorials centred on war and conflict. This is despite the fact that the history of women war correspondents working on stories from the field go way back to World War II.

If war and conflict reporting is a tough job for males, is

it tougher for females? Is that why reportedly, around 75 per cent war correspondents across the world are men and barely 25 per cent are women? Or is it because women have a dual responsibility of running the home and hearth and also covering war and conflict zones distanced from home and children? According to Chauhan, 'Female journalists have always found themselves confined to the so-called 'happy-go-merry' journalistic work and rarely enjoyed the golden opportunity to explore fields which are outside the ambit of desk reporting. It may be because our fairer sex is often considered weaker by their male counterparts. We all know journalism is rather a patriarchal profession. However, amidst all kinds of hardships and obstacles, some brave female journalists broke the ice and demonstrated exceptional courage in reporting from war fields, in the avatar of a war journalist. Here are top 7 female war journalists known for their exceptional courage.'

In India, there is immense scope for women journalists due to the terrible pockets of ethnic conflict that demand more women than men for reporting on live events because women and children in these pockets are forever in crisis situations that threaten their lives and homesteads. In these situations, women journalists would be more welcome than men under any circumstances. In this sense, the line that divides war reporting and conflict reporting is quite blurred in countries torn by ethnic conflict.

Abeer Saady is a well-known Egyptian journalist who imparts safety training to reporters working in hostile areas. In an event organized by International Association of Women in Radio and Television (IAWRT) in New Delhi, Saady in conversation with Baruah said, 'On my very first day as a reporter on 2 March 2013, I was attacked. I had gone to a New Delhi suburb after a seven-year-old girl had been raped inside a school. Outside the hospital, a mob of men pelted stones, vandalised shops and attacked TV broadcasting vans. My cameraperson and I were surrounded, beaten and abused. Over the course of that evening, I became the story. It's a pretty obvious rule of journalism and it's worth repeating—a journalist covering a story should not become the story,' in *Reporting Under Fire–Tales of Women Journalists in India* published by The Quint.

Baruah very rightly points out, 'The definition of conflict is not just war. It includes protests, rallies and angry mobs. Being in harm's way is an occupational hazard for a journalist.' Maya Mirchandani, Senior Editor, NDTV has over two decades of experience as a field reporter. In 1999, when she stopped to ask President Chandrika Kumaratunga in Sri Lanka a question, a bomb exploded 15 feet away, injuring both of them. She says one doesn't need to cover a war to be a target.

Suhasini Haidar has reported on conflicts in Pakistan, Sri Lanka, Syria, Lebanon, Libya and Tibet. In 2000, while reporting from Kashmir, she was injured when a car bomb exploded. Haider, who is now Diplomatic and Strategic Affairs Editor, *The Hindu*, in Delhi, says, 'Over a decade ago, when I covered Libya or the separatist movement in Kashmir, I was welcomed and even protected. Now there are radicalised groups like ISIS plugging extreme Islam. Journalists are now specific targets of terror groups.'

Reporting from rural India can also be termed 'conflict reporting' especially when women are involved in reporting as well as writing in and on these areas. Amrita Yadav of *The*

Hindu has reported from the eastern Indian state of Jharkhand, prone to violence by Maoist rebels. Jharkhand is also one of the most economically backward states of the country. 'When I am reporting, I am not worried about Naxal attacks,' says Yadav because 'They do not usually target reporters.'

Across the world, women were banned from the front lines until the US war on Vietnam, when a dozen of tough women journalists defied US military regulations and ventured to the front. Some of them earned recognition, but their male colleagues generally dismissed them as 'girl reporters.' Several were wounded and one, Georgette 'Dickey' Chapelle, a *National Geographic* photojournalist, was killed by a mine while on patrol with Marines outside Chu Lai on 4 November 1965. She was 46, and her martyrdom marked her as the first American female correspondent killed in action. Another similar martyr was Marie Colvin, who was killed in Syria in 2012.

There is no romance, glamour or aura associated with war and conflict reporting because it is fraught with danger at every step, sometimes mistaken for action and adventure. Death is a great equaliser in terms of gender and age, but for women, it is more dangerous because they face the fear of being raped, stripped, whipped, molested, mishandled and subjected to all kinds of violence that may not necessarily end in death.

In its 2001 report *Leading in a Different Language: Will Women Change the New Media?* the International Women's Media Foundation points out, 'Today, the majority of media companies world-wide are managed by men. While some women have advanced into media leadership, men make most of the decisions about what does and does not constitute as news. In addition, women are not moving into leadership positions in the media in numbers that reflect their numbers in society.'

'The power of media in warfare is formidable. It can be a mediator or an interpreter or even a facilitator of conflict. If only by editing away facts that do not fit the demands of air time or print space' state Elizabeth Rehan and Ellen Sirleaf in *Women, War and Peace*.

Though international and internal conflicts may differ in various aspects, their impacts on women's lives are similar. Thus, when talking about conflict zones, it is necessary to understand this expression as including internal conflicts as well. It is also essential to interpret the term 'internal conflicts' in its broad sense, encompassing situations that are not officially recognized by the respective States, nevertheless which due to their characteristics could be acknowledged as such. In fact, in many cases of internal armed conflict, governments refuse to admit the existence of a conflict situation to avoid the recognition of armed groups in fear of granting these groups legitimacy.

Does gender play any special role for women covering conflict and war zones that may be different for men than they may be for women? In their informative and illuminating article *Women War Correspondents: They Are Different in So Many Ways*, authors Anthony Feinstein and Mark Sinyor show how studies of tens of thousands of people from 17 countries demonstrate that geography is less salient than gender. Whether journalists live in the United States or Japan, Turkey or Taiwan, they are more likely to develop depression or anxiety if they are female. Female civilians in war-torn Kosovo, Sri Lanka, Yugoslavia, Nepal and Afghanistan also were found to have higher rates of depression and anxiety. Data collected by the US military show female soldiers to be more susceptible to psychological problems than their male counterparts.

A closer look at the data reveals that war photographers, for example, have higher rates of PTSD symptoms than print reporters or producers. And freelance journalists have more depression than peers who are employed by major news organizations. This has been seen likely to be more in women reporters than in men because of the double responsibilities they are burdened under.

Some reasons why women war and conflict journalists are likely to suffer more from stress and PTSD are pointed out as follows:

- Family responsibilities have an impact on the work of women journalists
- War and conflict reporting does not recognise their rights to maternity leave
- Promotional opportunities are affected by childcare
- They have to put up with sexist remarks and gestures from colleagues or sources
- They are subject to sexual harassment at work and war

For India's female journalists, it is a big leap from the way things were a few decades earlier, when women weren't even allowed to leave the office to report. Journalism in India was a male bastion in the 1940s and the 1950s, with the exception of a few women in newspaper offices, who usually wrote columns or worked on weekend editions but were almost never sent on reporting assignments by their male bosses.

The first woman to break the convention and make a mark in Indian journalism was the legendary photojournalist

Homai Vyarawalla who died in 2012. She began her career in the 1930s, covered major political events and personalities, and even photographed some events in World War II along with her photographer husband. She belonged to a time when photojournalism was a little known term in journalism and was almost exclusively a male occupation.

Posterity will never create another Homai Vyarawalla. She is one of the most low-profile but illustrious photojournalists India has ever produced. Her peak years as a photojournalist were from 1938 to 1970. The photographs she took of the first ever tricolour hoisting after Independence, the death of Mahatma Gandhi, Prime Minister Jawaharlal Nehru releasing a pigeon are now a part of the national archives. Her photographs narrate the story of India in the years leading up to Independence and during the confused but hopeful years after that. Draped in a Parsi-style sari and lugging her heavy camera equipment around, Vyarawalla was a familiar figure in Delhi. She captured some of the most passionate moments of a young nation while she tracked events that rewrote the history of modern India.

The late Prabha Dutt, mother of Barkha Dutt, who died several years ago, was the first female journalist to cover war in India. 'Her editors at *Hindustan Times* refused to send her,' says Usha Rai, a veteran woman journalist of many decades. But that did not stop Ms Dutt, who took leave from her office to go to the frontier and filed dispatches during the second war that India fought with Pakistan in 1965. The initial reports were ignored by her editors at the *Hindustan Times*, but gradually they were published because they were good.

Prabha's daughter Barkha Dutt, group editor with NDTV,

first shot to prominence for her detailed reportage of the Kargil War in 1999. She has been bestowed with Padma Shri, the fourth highest civilian honour of India. Having covered conflicts in Kashmir, Pakistan, Afghanistan and Iraq, she is better known for her in-depth coverage of the Kargil war that was fought between India and Pakistan. Her interview with the late Captain Vikram Batra strongly motivated her to take up journalism as a career.

Anne Sebba, a biographer and former Reuters correspondent in Rome, notes that in many ways, things are easier today for a woman reporter than they were in what she calls 'the days of the still-idolized Martha Gellhorn, who had to dress up as a hospital orderly in order to report the D-Day landings in competition with her husband Ernest Hemingway.'

On Gender, Media And Human Rights

SINCE THE 1960s, the women's movement has been engaged in a systematic and constant critique of media institutions and their output. Women's representation in the media helps to keep them in a position of relative powerlessness. The term 'symbolic annihilation,' coined by George Gerbner in 1972, became a powerful and widely used metaphor to describe the ways in which media images render women invisible. This 'mediated' invisibility is achieved not simply through the non-representation of women's points of view or perspectives on the world. When women are 'visible' in media content, the manner of their representation reflects the biases and assumptions of those who define the public—and therefore the media agenda. Despite measures to redress gender imbalances, the power to define public and media agendas is still mainly a male privilege.

The Gendered Politics of Knowledge

The separation between politics and knowledge is artificial and false. Politics is supposedly kept distanced from knowledge because the former is considered to be a source of contamination within the scheme of the structuring of knowledge. On the other hand, it is argued that political knowledge is essentially objective. If one probes a bit deeper, knowledge is deeply gendered in a patriarchal society at various levels as follows:

- What constitutes knowledge is decided by men of dominant sections of society. An example is the division of knowledge between theory and experience which claims that men's voice is theoretical and that women's voice is experiential.
- Most knowledge produced by men of dominant sections of society is generalised and passed as human knowledge. Dominant anthropology and history claims that men built civilisations. This has been accepted and acknowledged by major theoretical frameworks about human evolution. But feminists underscored the fact that women had discovered agriculture.
- Women are excluded from the process of knowledge and as subjects of knowledge. Any major text on Western political thought will throw up examples of how women are excluded while bestowing authorship.
- Women are almost always excluded as subjects of knowledge. For example, in any stratification study, the status of the household is marked by the economic status of the man, despite the statistical reality of around 60 per cent of Indian households being headed by females.

- Knowledge produced by women is labelled 'deviant'. For example, most women who were burnt to death during the medieval ages after being declared to be 'witches' were actually healers and early health guides. But these women were killed. Feminist historians raise questions about these killings being coincidental with the medical profession emerging as a profitable male profession with the blessings of the Church.

Patriarchy therefore established and perpetuated the myth that men make knowledge and women keep and maintain traditions.

The tragedy of Draupadi

The game of dice is the central episode in *Mahabharat*. The orchestration, choreography and script that builds up, sustains and establishes the game of dice is totally conceived, executed and dictated by patriarchy. When Vidura has a premonition that something terrible is going to happen even before the invitations are sent out, Dhritarashtra says: 'Do not worry. Nothing untoward will happen in my presence and in the presence of Bhishma.' Thus, whatever happens is seen as part of 'the divine plan.' Duryodhana escapes the responsibility of his actions by saying: 'One and only One governs all actions and the script of governance is in place even before the human being is born. It is He whose commands I am following.'

Draupadi's *vastra-haran* in the court in full view of everyone present is the worst violation of human rights imaginable; the sole voice of doubt is that of Vikarna who asks: 'Are we truly conducting ourselves in accordance with Dharma?' But Karna snubs him at once. 'All these men, do you think they know nothing?' Draupadi stands for no more than a 'symbol' of honour of the Pandavas; her body is a blank page on which scripts of revenge and humiliation, the story of men fighting like a pack of dogs are written; when she raises the question of whether a lady of the royal family deserves this treatment, Duryodhana says that she deserves this treatment precisely because she is a lady from the royal family. She has to be humiliated because she is the 'woman' of the enemy. Thus, she is denied all agency and individuality.

Contemporary poet Suman Kesahri imagines what the original author denied Draupadi by stating what Draupadi would have said had the author given her a voice. 'Draupadi, Panchali, Krishna, Yajnaseni—all of these are adjectives, none of them is a noun. Did it ever strike you that I have no name? I had only raised some questions, I only had some queries. And you have taken away even my name!'

Curfew is a kind of violence

In the mid-Eighties, when Ahmedabad was caught in the trap of violent riots, the media completely missed out on the debilitating impact of the curfew on the lives of ordinary citizens, particularly the poor, who cannot afford to stock up on provisions. (Ammu Joseph, January 2004.) During the riots and after, curfew was imposed round the clock, often for as long as seven to ten days at a stretch, at times even touching the maximum permissible limit of 500 hours. It forced large families to survive for days on the meagre provisions they happened to have at home when curfew was announced—often at the dead of night. The entire onus of managing the difficult situation, of feeding hungry families with nothing beyond onions, gram and wheat flour, of pacifying wailing children with black tea fell on the women.

The media missed out on these stories because they had not talked to women, especially poor women in the affected areas. Their reports were based on information and analysis gleaned from 'authorities,' 'leaders' of various groups and sundry 'experts.' The tendency was to dismiss the imposition and relaxation of curfew with a single, bland sentence or none at all. Talking to women actually suffering due to the curfew would perhaps have worked as persuasion to the authorities concerned to devise practical solutions to solve the problems of common people suffering for no fault of their own.

In the 1980s, an estimated 29-33 per cent of the women organised by SEWA were sole supporters of their families; a substantial percentage of the rest earned more than the male members; it could be easily understood that a major slice of the women's incomes went towards meeting the basic needs of their families whereas a substantial portion of the men's earnings is often spent on drinking, smoking and gambling. So, women's loss of income during the five months of trouble proved disastrous for a large number of families. As a result of this media 'invisibility', the relief work of the government did not consider the loss of livelihood suffered by thousands of women working in the informal sector. Their families therefore, did not receive the kind of help they needed to survive in the short term, and to rebuild their lives in the long term.

Media representations in general, and of women in particular, are deeply embedded in political and economic contexts. Studies from India point to the often-contradictory ways in which the media and advertising are compromising women's multiple identities in contemporary society. Images of the 'new woman' as an independent consumer whose femininity remains intact, or as a hard-headed individualist whose feminine side must be sacrificed, illustrate new stereotypes of women whose 'femaleness' is always the core issue.

These findings and others clearly illustrate that despite the small shifts noted in retrospective analyses, the media content, by and large, still reflects a masculine vision of the world. A wide-scale social and political transformation, in which women's rights—and women's right to communicate—are truly understood, respected and implemented both in society at large and by the media needs emphasis. The manipulation of gender images by male-dominated media should make us critically examine what we see every day on TV, in magazines and newspapers. Global media-monitoring programmes undertaken by different groups in different countries show that nothing much has changed over the years. The same misrepresentations and stereotypes persist. Women continue to be marginalised.

On the one hand, by endorsing a few liberal reforms like equal pay, the media reinforces the message that women have every right to expect to be treated as equal citizens, with the same rights, responsibilities, and opportunities as men. On the other hand, by mocking and dismissing the way feminist activists look, dress, behave and talk, the media also endorses the notion that in some cases, female subordination and sexual objectification were not only fine but desirable as well.

The contradiction, sanctioning the notion of women as autonomous and equal citizens while also endorsing the idea that women are around to be gazed at (advertisements, beauty contests, fashion parades, film), is the contradiction that lessened women's potential then and has the same effect today. Although the media did foster the spread of the liberation movement through its vast coverage, the media also hampered the movement's potential and women's potential as individuals by placing female attractiveness at the forefront.

While gender is often seen as a narrow, special interest issue, gender awareness can lead to a better, more holistic understanding of any situation.

The Gender Revolution In Film Posters
From Mother India To Kahaani

FILM POSTERS OFFER subliminal messages that sometimes reach beyond the film. They throw the 'first look' before a film's release as teasers to attract the audience. In male-dominated cinema, most posters are generally plastered with faces of the hero. Even if the heroine has a stronger role, she is relegated to a marginal position in the poster. But what happens when the woman is almost an exclusive presence in a film and the men are rendered unimportant, like Mehboob's *Mother India*?

Mehboob had a gender-free agenda when it came to posters of his films. For *Aan* (1952), he introduced Nadira as the leading lady of a film that thematically followed the lines of Shakespeare's *The Taming of the Shrew*. Though the hero of the film was the heart-stopping Dilip Kumar, a top star of the time, the posters feature a prominent and expressive close-up of Nadira sharing space with her hero.

Mother India marks a turning point in the shift in emphasis from hero to leading lady. Earlier on, when the leading lady dominated the story, she shared poster space with the hero. Though the title *Patita* (1953) spells out that the story focusses on the heroine, the poster gives Usha Kiron less space than it gives to Dev Anand. The same applies to *Pakeezah* (1972), named after the character Meena Kumari portrayed. The posters give prominent space to the heroine but also feature a big close-up of hero Raaj Kumar's face. In one of the posters of Guru Dutt's *Sahib Bibi Aur Ghulam* (1962), Meena Kumari who played the major role of Chhoti Bahu, finds predominance on the posters. But we also see a close-up of Guru Dutt complemented with two small visages of Rehman and Waheeda Rehman in the backdrop.

The scenario changed dramatically with Prakash Jha's *Mrityudand* (1997). The story that revolves around the struggles of three different women against the patriarchal structure of a village where women are used, misused and abused by the men, Jha's poster was designed to position the three women in close-up towering over a crowd of dwarfed men cowering under their shadow. The main poster of Mahesh Manjrekar's *Astitva* (2000) shows one half of the face of the protagonist portrayed by Tabu, prominently cutting Sachin Kherdekar out of the frame. The half face spells out the significance of the leading lady's 'existence' (*astitva*) reduced to half her value and potential within a marriage that never was.

Jism (2003), that claimed to be an erotic thriller, explored the woman's assertion of her sexuality with no holds barred. The body of the woman was on grand display through her clothes and the lack of them in different degrees of the sensual and the sexual. The posters reflected the passion of the woman and the man occupied secondary position. Some posters featured Bipasha Basu alone occupying the entire poster. This would have been unthinkable for any publicity machinery even ten years ago.

Aitraaz (2004) directed by Abbas-Mastaan had the posters designed keeping the *femme fatale* played by Priyanka Chopra as the dominating character in the film who is a mind-blowing seducer and game-planner and lives and even dies strictly on her own terms. Kareena Kapoor is also present in some posters but Akshay Kumar is marginalised. *7 Khoon Maaf* (2011) is another classic example.

In the posters of *Ishqiyan* (2010), Vidya Balan plays the mysterious Krishna. She believes she is a widow but that does not stop her from seducing the two men—an uncle and his nephew—primarily to fulfill her sexual needs and partly to grind some self-serving axe. Posters of her films are a strong reflection of this powerful aura of a woman. Raj Kumar Gupta's *No One Killed Jessica* (2011) based on the quest for justice on the real life story of Jessica Lal has no hero. The two women characters portrayed by Rani Mukherjee and Vidya Balan complement and counterpoint each other and the posters of the film lucidly spell this out.

Milan Luthria's *The Dirty Picture* (2011) is loosely adapted from the tragic story of the southern actress Silk Smitha. Silk made celluloid sleaze and her real-life romps with several men a fashion statement takes the cake where Vidya, portraying Silk on screen, sets the screen on fire without appearing vulgar, cleavage on prominent display. Most posters focus on her deep cleavage, acquired exclusively for her role, surrounded by the greedy men in her life. It is not for nothing that the role brought her a string of awards and endless appreciation from the mass audience and from critics.

Kahaani (2012) turns the ideological principle *Mother India* on its head. One significant poster sheds light on a different kind of twenty-first century 'Durga'. It shows her with ten hands and a pregnant bump but without the third eye. It reflects that Durga, the Mother Goddess who destroyed Mahisasura in the mythological tale, has changed in this century. She is a computer engineer trained and skilled in killing people. She pursues her enemy with diabolic planning, and is neither pregnant nor a mother. Milan Luthra played around with a sensitive religious icon like Durga and this film became one of the biggest hits of the year.

My Choice Or No Choice?

MA DURGA COMES on her annual visit to Planet Earth with children in tow. We place her on a pedestal and worship her for five days only to dump her in the water on the last day, not bothering what happens to the remains of the clay, the bamboo, the straw and the paint that fleshed her out in the first place. So, we do not give her a choice about how she will go back or whether she would like to stay on for some more time. She has the rigidly fixed five days of holidays to stand on that high pedestal we place her on and watch worshippers queue every morning and night to pray to her. No one cares if she feels tired on that high perch and would perhaps like to rest for a while. She has to wait for her *bhog* till the umpteenth Anajli is over and the curtain is drawn in front of her so that no one can watch her eat. What if she wants to sit along with her devotees and share her *bhog* with them?

It is no surprise, therefore, that someone with the grey cells in the right place decided to run a campaign to showcase one actress who insists she lives life on her own terms. Let us take a closer look.

Will the My Choice video really reach the target audience—women everywhere and impress them enough to empower them? True empowerment comes from contributing towards making society better. Please note that the empowerment video has been created, conceived and directed by a man—Homi Adajania—famous for his ad commercials. Agreed that many men have a deep perception of the woman question within patriarchy but this video has a commercial purpose and not a social or philanthropic one. It may be a public service campaign but behind the 'public service' are the hidden tax waivers the participants in the video including Deepika Padukone, one of the highest paid actresses in Bollywood today, will benefit from. 'What happens when 99 women from varying walks of life come together to send out one powerful message?' goes the tagline above the video. Do these 99 women represent 60 crore of the Indian population?

A feedback from Vivek Chetri points out that it is demeaning for a woman that in this entire video on 'woman empowerment', the only choices they talk about are clothes and sex. 'Isn't there more to life than this? It seems more like an effort to catch eyeballs than to seriously talk about women's empowerment,' he says.

Another insightful comment comes from Sampad Dutt, 'The video for me displays the highest order of pretence and pseudo feminism,' he points out. 'It openly advocates infidelity and adultery as a means of empowerment. Empowerment means both men and women getting equal and just opportunities to live and prosper. Deepika says: "My choice. To be a size 0 or a size 15. They don't have a size for my spirit, and never will…" This is the same person who suggests a breakfast cereal so that women look "special" in the wedding season. The double standards are quite obvious,' he writes.

The women featured in the video are either models or celebrities in some field or another. Most of them are very photogenic and camera-friendly—familiar, high-profile faces. Some token lip service has been paid to the ordinary woman through a wrinkled face peeping from between the other faces or a rural woman in colourful costume and jewellery probably borrowed from tourism posters or calendars or designed separately for this given video. It does not matter. But they are immobile faces, stationary with a fixed expression for women who might never have the good fortune of watching the finished product. Why no fat women, no very dark and plain looking women, no ordinary women off the streets, no skeletal, hungry-looking women, no little girls from the pavements of cities or outside their village hutments, no anonymous faces gracing My Choice?

Should one therefore deduce that these women do not have choice? This is the basic truth the video is unwittingly making. Choices are only for women like Padukone and her friends in the video and for women like us who raise our voices on social networking sites to draw attention and not for the maid who works in my house or the sweeper who sweeps the roads in front of my residence or the woman who gathers the waste from the bins everyday. Choice is not for the sex workers who line the bridge near the Kalighat crematorium every evening waiting to get a customer for their daily bread. Choice is not for the peasant woman or the daily labourer at the construction site who takes her kids to work because there is nowhere to leave them and no school to send them to. Choice is not for the vegetable vendor or the vessel seller or the bricklayer who has no clue where the next meal will come from. But then, they will not be watching the video anyway.

In its simplest form, power is defined as 'a person's ability to control or change the behaviour of others and the ability to realise his/her will against opposition.' Extending this logic to include women, a woman's power is defined as her ability to control and change other people's behaviour and also to determine important events in their lives, even when others are opposed to these changes. Do women have this power? It has nothing to do with 'choice' as the video claims. Women are not empowered in patriarchal and patrilineal societies where men hold everything in absolute control. However, in many cases, the power question is disguised very cleverly with these so-called 'empowerment' videos like 'My Choice' so that women are made to feel that they are powerful, even when they are not. This is achieved within patriarchy for the convenience of its 'safe' and continuous sustenance through time and place. This does not seem a difficult task because it is very difficult to determine at what point exactly there is a social equality between men and women in any society.

Terms like My Choice, empowerment, disempowerment and equality mean nothing to 70 per cent of the children. Poverty is becoming a women's issue. Nearly six in ten poor adults are women, and nearly six in ten poor children live in families headed by women. Poverty rates are especially high for single mothers, women of colour and elderly women living alone. For them, even living is not a choice and dying is inevitable. The feminisation of poverty is a term used to describe the overwhelming representation of women among the poor. 'Women tend to be disproportionately represented among the poor…the poorer the family the more likely it is to be headed by a women'. So, does the word 'choice' exist in her dictionary? Has she ever heard of it? Does size zero, even when explained, make sense to women who are destined to remain size zero and die size zero?

Kiran Sharma, in her paper '*Women, Poverty and Food Security in India*' writes: 'Households are not homogenous entities, since within a household, women and girl children often tend to be relatively more undernourished. Gender constitutes the most profound differentiating division. A gendered analysis of poverty reveals not simply its unequal incidence but also that both cause and effect are deeply gendered. Women face a greater risk of poverty than men.' What kind of choice will Homi Adajania, Vogue Empowerment along with his 99 high-powered models offer these poverty-ridden women?

Documentary filmmaker Sonali Gulati has come up with an awesome video called 'Rewrite' in which, through a long poem, she breaks down each myth of women empowerment of My Choice propagated by the video which, she strongly insists, actually is disempowerment. Somewhere in the middle, she states:

> *You are the FAKE, who wants to MAKE*
> *A video about women*
> *by exoticising and fetishising*
> *and copywriting from within your shit storm*
> *And no please don't bother waking up*
> *Keep sleeping and keep dreaming*

of your Vogue-worthy women
with their hair flying in slow motion
just like all the other advertising bullshit that you do

More damning is the insight by Hina Ali who says, 'There are many software applications available that can increase the "likes" to the video on its website.' She adds the interesting fact that after 500 responses on the website, *Vogue* turned off the reply button because most of the reviews were horrible. 'I have been following this since the day it began and suddenly I found 5000k likes increased within a few minutes. So there has been some tampering for sure.'

So, whose Choice are we talking about anyway: Yours, mine, Deepika Padukone's or Homi's, who conceived of idea in the first place?

When Reel Meets Real
Gulab Gang Vs Gulabi Gang

THERE IS A trend in Hindi mainstream cinema to make biopics of real-life heroes, *Bhag Milkha Bhag* being an example. It is a fictionalised account of the life of Olympic athlete Milkha Singh. However, besides targeting the mass audience with its three-pronged functions of education, information and entertainment, the film has a fourth dimension—to inspire and influence our youngsters. This is a glamourised story of one of the greatest athletes India has produced.

What happens when a producer-director makes a film on a real 'movement'? Does the glamourisation of a flesh-and-blood movement by women against violation of human rights through a mainstream *masala* film add to the cause of these women? Or does it take away by trivialising the movement through the film? Are producer Anubhav Sinha and debutant director Shoumik Sen trying to capitalise a real rural women's movement through their film *Gulab Gang*? Conceptualising a celluloid representation of an individual achiever like Milkha Singh or Mary Kom is a different story. But riding piggyback on a collective movement striving to fight for the rights of the deprived, the oppressed and the poor, both men and women, is another cup of tea.

Let us take a brief look at Gulabi Gang. Founded by Sampat Pal Devi, 43, an unlettered mother of five in 2006, Gulabi Gang now has a strength of thousands rural women clad in pink saris journeying from one town to another in Bundelkhand district in Uttar Pradesh to create awareness among poor and neglected men and women about their rights and to fight for rights that have already been violated, or try and bring justice to victims who are no more. Sampat Pal was married to an ice-cream vendor when she was 12 and had her first child when she was 15.

Once, in 2006, Sampat Pal saw a man beating up his wife brutally; no one turned a hair because domestic violence was a given in Bundelkhand and both men and women had internalised it. Sampat Devi appealed to the husband to stop beating his wife. But the man abused her right back. She came back the next morning with five other women armed with a thick stick and beat up this man till he began to beg for mercy. The news of five women beating up one man spread like wildfire and women from neighbouring villages soon came to her asking for help. She asked most of them to join in and Gulabi Gang was born. 'The colour pink does not have any religious or political association and is neutral in every way. Therefore, we chose pink and took the colour as part of the name of our ever-expanding group,' says Sampat Pal.

Gulabi Gang has stopped several child marriages, forced

the police to register domestic violence cases and marked out the dowry death of a young woman which the in-laws, with the connivance of the police, passed off as 'suicide.' The families initially do not like their women to become social activists in a real sense but they come around in course of time. There are a few exceptions when a woman drops out because a family member is a part of the investigation. The group, which the Indian media portrayed positively, was reported to have 20,000 members till 2008, as well as a chapter in Paris, France.

This is the Gulabi Gang that has inspired several documentary filmmakers to make a film on their grassroots activism that is moving from one success to another. On the other side of the coin, *Gulab Gang* is a feature film with Madhuri Dixit portraying the leader of a woman's group, perhaps trying to impose a beautiful face on the ordinary and rustic but gutsy Sampat Pal. While exploring the news reports appearing about *Gulab Gang*, the ethics of this celluloid 'imitation' came up. Let us ask ourselves what ethics lies behind hijacking and appropriating real life stories for feature films and capitalising on important and positive movements by diverting attention from the real cause to synthetic glamour.

Documentary filmmaker Nishtha Jain, whose *Gulabi Gang* won the Best Film Award in Muhr Asia Africa documentary section at the ninth Dubai Film Festival followed by a string of awards and nominations says, 'I found Sampat Pal amazing. She is completely self-taught and had the courage to break away from her in-laws to do the work she's doing now. I thought if these women, despite all their disadvantages, can rise against injustice, so can anyone. It would be an inspiring tale to tell. So I decided to go and meet Sampat Pal. Within days of observing her at work, I realised that reality was more complicated than I thought that it would make for a more nuanced film.'

Gulabi Gang is a collective movement spearheaded by Sampat Pal. *Gulab Gang* is a commercial film. One journalist reports, 'Madhuri Dixit portrays the character of Rajjo who heads Gulabi Gang, a group of women dacoits dressed in pink saris that operates in the Bundelkhand region. The audience will get to see Madhuri in a rough, abusive and action-packed performance unlike her other roles that have been very feminine and demure in nature.' So, a group of gutsy women have been turned into 'dacoits' with a single twist of the scriptwriter's pen! What kind of justice will this bring to Sampat Pal and her Gulabi Gang? Another unnamed source says, 'She (Madhuri Dixit) has worked with a team of professionals with whom she has learnt kick-boxing and high kicks moves for the film.' She reportedly trained under Shaolin master Shifu Kanishka Sharma.

However, perhaps scared of reprisals from the media specially from the people of Bundelkhand in general and the women of Gulabi Gang in particular, the producer-director duo of Anubhav Sinha and Shoumik Sen have retracted from earlier stories in the media about the film being a celluloid representation of Gulabi Gang. Earlier this month, Anubhav Sinha said that his debut production venture *Gulab Gang* is not based on any real-life character contradicting all earlier stories about it being loosely based on activist Sampat Pal and her Gulabi Gang. However, Sinha cleared the air through his tweet and wrote: 'For the record, *Gulab Gang* is fiction. Not based on anyone's life, loosely or tightly.'

The question that remains is—if the film has nothing to do with anyone's life, then why call the film *Gulabi Gang* and why make the women wear pink? And why is it set against the backdrop of Bundelkhand, where the real Gulabi Gang was born and is the base of the movement?

Bundelkhand in central India, a region notorious for its rebels-turned-armed bandits, is witnessing a new kind of rebellion with an unusual cast of characters. Bundelkhand is marked among the poorest of the poor in the district. Will this fit into the synthetic scenario of a Bollywood film?

Using the name and the colour of the group and placing the story in Bundelkhand to tell a different story is not only unfair and unethical, it is also against the morals that guide and rule creative artistic expression through a mass medium of entertainment like cinema. Instead of contributing to the real movement, it is likely to send across the wrong message to the right people every time!

Was *Gulab Gang* a tribute to the real Gulabi Gang? Or is it a travesty of faith in cinema's ability to tell real stories in fictionalised form? It is best left to the viewers to judge. For me, it is a trivialising of a serious movement through the language of mainstream Bollywood.

Saankal
A Bizarre Tale Of A Social Custom

EVEN A BADLY made film that got invited to several film festivals becomes a learning experience for the viewer because it sheds light on little known human rights violations in the name of tradition.

Saankal (Hindi) is a film that is a classic example of strong content marred by bad making. But it scores in terms of shedding light on a cruel custom that is still practised by Meher Muslims in villages in Rajasthan's Jaisalmer and Barmer districts.

Directed by debutant director Dedpiya Joshi, *Saankal* which means 'shackle' brings across the terrible truth of unmarried girls remaining spinsters as there were no eligible bridegrooms. Men, however, are allowed to marry outside the faith, making it more difficult to find grooms.

Why? The director says, 'After 1947, during the Partition of India into India and Pakistan, some Indian villages became a part of Western Pakistan. Marriages were arranged between families on either side for some time. But after a few years, government interventions built impossible-to-cross blocks and families on both sides lost complete control over connections with their relatives across the border. Consequently, the number of marriageable males went down and more and more growing girls did not get married for want of eligible young men. The option left for these unmarried girls, considered to be a social stigma for the families they belonged to, was either to remain spinsters or to marry very old men who died soon after.

By the time the village council realised the disaster, it was too late. Instead of uprooting the cause, they passed another law in panic which they felt would be a solution to the problem—they decided to get these girls married off to small boys in matching families. This worsened the position of both bride and groom instead of resolving the problem.

This meant that a girl of twenty-six was married against her will to a boy of eleven. That is just half the story because this tale has an ugly, incredible twist. The young bride in the film is persistently raped by men in her husband's family including the boy's father, uncles and so on with the tacit support of women in the same family. But there are problems. When the girl gets pregnant, who would be considered the father of the baby? What would happen to the baby and the bride herself? Going back to her parents was unthinkable within the community. She has to do backbreaking work during the day and at night, men would enter the bedroom and rape her one after another.

Saankal narrates the story of one girl who grows to love her boy-husband as he grows up but who cannot rescue her from her torture. She commits suicide. The story sounds very powerful but the film is weak in terms of performance, presentation, music, acting and technique. The best thing about the film is its subject matter and the picturesque backdrops. Kids like Kesar and young girls like Abeera became victims of this malpractice. The director and his entire team have tried their best to convey the evil effects of this tradition through the film.

However, authenticity and research have been sacrificed in favour of 'glamour'. The debutant heroine who portrays the main victim does not look like a rural Rajasthani girl with rustic features. She has neatly plucked eyebrows and wears colourful dresses that sound a false note whenever she appears on screen. For this story filled with pain and tragedy, one fails to understand why the director and his team chose a mainstream strategy to deliver an off track plot and theme.

This custom came to light in an enlightening article by Rohit Parihar titled *Burdened by custom* in *India Today*. But neither did the readers or any NGO pick up the story and work towards its elimination nor did the governments at the village, district or regional level do anything about it.

Politically speaking, the administration at the regional state level is afraid of losing out on vote banks by trying to curb traditional customs that are a violation of human rights not only of young women but also of the boy child who does not understand the implications and responsibilities that marriage brings.

The ghettoes inhabited by Meher Muslims are Revari village on the Jaisalmer-Barmer highway, Nimba ki Basti village of Jaisalmer district and Bachhe ki Dhani village where a girl, unable to put up with the situation, committed suicide. Though the father-in-law was charged with abetment to suicide, he was subsequently released for lack of evidence. Such marriages are in blatant violation of the Child Marriage Restraint Act, 1929, (revised in 1978) the police chooses to turn a blind eye.

According to Act, the minimum legal age for marriage stands at eighteen years for girls and twenty-one years for men. Thus even boys have the right not to be married at a young age.

Both husband and wife are victims of a practice that has long outlived its need and utility within the community even if it had any to begin with. But who is listening?

Sankaal depicts how tradition can bring a drastic change in normal life. In middle of the Thar desert, here is a village that has evolved its own rituals, taboos and social obligations. The idea behind the custom was to maintain purity of the bloodline. Any divergence resulted in violence.

Tanima Bhattacharya, who portrays the older wife in *Saankal*, her debut film, has won the Best Female Lead award at the Indie Gathering at Cleveland, Ohio, USA in 2015 along with the film bagging the Best Foreign Film Award. She went on to win the Best Actress Award at the Online Russian International Film Festival in October 2015 while the film won the Best Film Award.

The Shaan-e-Awadh International Film Festival, Lucknow in November 2015, bestowed three awards to the film—Best Film, Best Actress and Best Director. Other awards are the Golden Award in the Foreign Film Competition category at California in January 2016, the Best Story Prize from the Kalyan International Film Festival, Maharashtra in February 2016 and the Best Film in the Women's Section at the DFW Dallas South Asian Film Festival the same month and year.

Many very badly made Indian films are bagging awards at

film festivals in India and beyond borders even though they do not reach anywhere in terms of the craft of cinema such as story-telling, cinematography, editing, framing and most importantly, acting.

Saankal is a classic case in point. But the questions that get raised in this context that also provide the answers are—Do the films win in terms of the strong content they advocate, until then little known to festival juries across the world? Or, are the festivals themselves too marginal and invisible, where better films do not take part and big banners do not evince a keenness to participate?

There are other films that do not merit even a release, much less a viewing. One example is *Alo Chhaya* (2014) where the director Ananya Samanta has claimed to place on celluloid Sarat Chandra Chatterjee's last short story. This story, however, turned out to be twisted completely out of shape in a story of love reincarnated and reborn. It dealt with the sub-plot of a widow's love for a young zamindar and won many awards at international film festivals; but was a very badly made film.

Another film *Hemalkasa* (Hindi) based on the life of Baba Amte and his wife who lived all their lives in Hemalkasa won the runner-up audience award at the London Indian Film Festival in 2014. It was also shortlisted among 300 films across the globe for the Best Foreign Film Award at the Academy Awards in 2015. It was a very positive film with strong content but had a very loosely created script and in spite of good performances by the two leads, could not be evaluated as a good film because the film craft was not up to the mark.

Madhurita Anand's film *Kajariya* (2013) that dealt with infanticide and a woman forced to pretend to be a witch to kill female infants, had a strong subject but the film released recently in India for a very short run. Apparently, it was made to appeal to foreign film festivals. It was among the three films that premiered in the Dubai International Film Festival in December 2013. It is a very shoddily made film that revealed the director's focus more on festival screenings and less on the quality of the film per se.

Film festivals are mushrooming by the dozen every day and you can see a festival of films at any nook and corner of any city or even suburb. There is no guarantee; however, that these festivals will raise their standards in the future or even that they will be able to sustain themselves over time. Many of the festival organisers are fly-by-night operators who are here today, gone tomorrow. The same applies to many of the production houses that send their films to participate in these festivals. Are these awards 'bought'? Or are they really 'won' on merit? These are questions that perhaps demand to be explored in greater depth. Many organisers of film festivals begin with the aim of rubbing shoulders with the glitterati, with the aim of making quick money through sponsorships drawn to festivals by the degree of 'glamour' they offer.

In the meantime, let us remain satisfied with content. As this writer mentioned at the outset—there is so much to learn.

Mai Ghat
Crime Number 103/2005

It's tough to make a feature film based on a true incident, especially when the director chooses to draw from a real-life court case. But actor-turned-director Ananth Mahadevan has done it before and he has done it once again with his new film *Mai Ghat – Crime No.103/2005* in Marathi. The film won the Hiralal Sen Memorial Award for Best Film at the 25 Kolkata International Film Festival recently.

On 24 July 2018, in a historic verdict, the CBI awarded two serving officers the death penalty, believed to be the first in India. *Mai Ghat – Crime No. 103/2005* tells us the back story of this sentence. The original incident happened in the South but Mahadevan has shifted it to Maharashtra.

The film opens in flashback mode and ends in the same way but you get to know this only when the film returns to where it began—the prematurely aged mother Prabha Mai (Usha Jadhav) sitting quietly on the steps of her home watching a crow trying to catch some crumbs on the steps. She looks on with a tired, resigned expression on her face.

The story unfolds between these two frames as the camera flashes back by 13 years when Prabha Mai's only teenaged son Nitin, who eked out a living through collection and selling of scrap, is arrested on a false charge of theft. In reality however, it is the police constable Sable (Kamlesh Sawant) who snatches Rs 4,200 Nitin is carrying to buy new clothes for the Marathi New Year.

When Nitin calls the policeman a thief, the policeman arrests him along with his friend Suresh without a warrant, releases Suresh after bashing him up badly and tortures Nitin so much that the boy dies within three hours of continuous torture.

All documented traces of the killing are wiped clean and the dead body is thrown on the *ghat* of a river and that is how Prabha Mai learns of her son's death. Prabha Mai is a single mother whose husband has left the family. He arrives on hearing of his son's death which has been reported as an 'accident', voicing hopes of a handsome 'compensation.' Prabha Mai remains silent and we never see the man again.

In fact, silence is her language, strategy, weapon of attack and defense and she expresses this silence in many ways— through her daily work of washing clothes of the town's people on the *ghat*, putting them out to dry on the clothesline, ironing them out on the antique, very heavy, coal-heated iron, doing her daily household chores and mostly, hiding her simmering anger around the injustice of her son's murder. What comes across powerfully through her body language and the fleeting expressions on her face is the quiet determination to see the two policemen who killed her older son hanged to death.

When any hope of justice seems to fade, she gets help from Ranjana (Suhasini Mulay), an aged lawyer who helps her move the case to CBI when witnesses back away and the lower court dismisses the case.

The film stands out also because of the ambience the director has created where Nature and the physical environment of the village/small town are juxtaposed against each other. The *ghat* where Mai washes her clothes, takes a dip and feels purified stands in contrast to the ghost of a city with its narrow roads, small shops and simple police station defining poverty and want while the *ghat* stands out in its sheer beauty even when the rains lash down on it or a fading sun peeps through a gap in the clouds.

Sable's cruel nature comes across when, at the sugarcane juice shop, he overturns his empty glass and traps an ant in it. He also refuses to pay the juice seller and tells him to add it to his dues. But he loves his daughter dearly and encourages her to play hockey. The CBI lawyer (Girish Oak) is sympathetic but practical and succeeds in convincing the lady constable Sunanda (Vibhavari Joshi) to become a witness for the defence at the risk of losing her job. Joshi portrays the role with a dignity rare among a crowd of male colleagues and boss. Ranjana, the senior lady lawyer, tells her to quickly choose between continuing in a men's toilet (the police station) and opting out.

The film is shot in almost monochromatic shades and one can hardly discern snatches of colour to match the drab life of Mai and her younger son, Ganesh. This boy once brings an antique Ganesha statue with an umbrella from scrap. Mai says she will take it inside the house only after she wins the case.

Once, Sable in mufti visits her to threaten her but she quietly continues to fold her *paan*. As she sticks it into her mouth, she says he is not only cruel but also stupid and stupid men can be very cruel.

The very young and relatively new actor Usha Jadhav has enough commanding presence to carry the entire film on her slender shoulders and hold her own even when pitted against veteran performers like Girish Oak and Suhasini Mulay. She slowly walks out of the courtroom when a witness describes in graphic detail how her son died. But we do not see her weeping or crying or sobbing for the entire length of the film.

The acting by the entire cast is almost organic, the credit for which must be shared between the director and his cast. The courtroom is completely stripped of glamour and all is orchestrated like a real court. The film makes minimum use for understated music that does not intrude into or lighten the gravity of the subject.

The sole point of relief comes in the brief interactions between Mai and her younger son Ganesh, 12 when Nitin dies and then around 25 when he comes back from his hostel on vacation. He brings the Ganesha idol in even before the court verdict is out. He urges his mother to slow down on her washing and to keep a helper but she remains quiet. In the end, we see her collecting all kinds of colourful clothes out of an old trunk, taking these to the *ghat* and arranging them to create the face of her dear son Nitin captured beautifully in a top angle shot. She pats that big face as if trying to put him to sleep.

The most outstanding feature of the entire film is the way in which Mahadevan has used restraint so that not for a single minute does a frame or scene go overboard or get into melodramatic mode though, given the narrative, there was enough scope for the film reducing itself into a tear-jerking melodrama. The actual torture and death in police custody is only through description and never through visuals.

Towards the end, Sable's wife and daughter visit Mai, begging her to forgive her husband. When Mai remains silent, reminding them of their absence for 13 long years, the woman, very angry, says, 'You are not fighting for justice, you are fighting for revenge.' Mai says, 'I have forgotten the difference between justice and revenge long back.'

There are two kinds of courage this film underlines—one is the subject of the film that demanded a lot of courage as it deals with a sharp and open indictment of the police and the other is the courage expressed by the protagonist drawn from the angst and pain of a mother who lost her son in real life.

The Housewife As A Prostitute

WHEN A FULL-TIME housewife becomes a sex worker, is she committing adultery or is she into a profession that makes her a financially independent woman? Does she step into the profession for money or is she looking for sex because she is deprived of a normal sex life within marriage? Is she sexually promiscuous or is her husband impotent?

Pratim D Gupta, the young film critic who wrote and directed *Shaheb Bibi Golaam* (Bengali) has addressed some of these very pertinent questions through one of the three pivotal characters in the film. The 'Bibi' in the film addressed first as Jaya, the housewife who is eventually christened Shuktara when she becomes a high-profile sex worker in a well-appointed Kolkata bordello located in a seedy bylane. The bordello is called The Housewives Club because its members are housewives from upper middle class families. There is no coercion involved and women step into the trade knowing fully well what they are getting into.

Shuktara is the Bengali equivalent of the Pole Star that shines brightly even on very dark nights and is clearly visible from earth. Gupta tries to blur the socially distinct lines drawn between the housewife and the sex worker. The two identities—being a housewife and also a sex worker—need not be mutually exclusive identities and may in fact, merge in the same person as it does in this film. Jaya enjoys her clandestine identity as Shuktara and loves the different men who come to her as clients, even if just for one night. She also enjoys being a mother to her loving daughter. She is wearied of being the criticised daughter-in-law, the taken-for-granted wife and the sexually deprived marriage partner.

Millions of Indian housewives remain silent about the complete lack of sex in their marriage after the first child is born. Most husbands—modern, urban, educated, young, successful and independent—forget that their wives need sexual fulfilment as much as they do. Mahesh Manjrekar tried to drive this point home in *Astitva*. Physical desire is hardly mentioned when it comes to married women. This collective conspiracy of silence allows them to be exploited without even being aware that sexual deprivation is also a kind of exploitation and humiliation of the mind and the body. In *Shaheb Bibi Golaam*, in one scene, a young male teacher of Jaya's daughter calls her for some issues relating to the child. Jaya discovers however, that it was just a ruse to touch her. When another young mother asks her to lodge a complaint, Jaya says, 'I rather liked the touch of a man after a long time.' This friend then takes her to the lane that introduces Jaya to another life.

The seeds of a housewife becoming a sex worker without disrupting the harmony of her normal role as wife and mother were laid by Basu Bhattacharya in *Aastha* (*In The Prison of Spring*, 1996). The 'inspiration' for *Aastha* is Goddard's much-discussed *Deux ou trois choses que je sais d'elle* (1966) where Juliette (Marina Vlady) is a working class housewife who becomes a prostitute in order to buy consumer goods for herself and her family. She thus condenses into a single figure—a metaphorical analogy of commodity and metonymy, shopping. But here is where the 'similarity' between Goddard's and Bhattacharya's films ends.

Mansi (Rekha) does not shop to produce the desirable surface, the 'look' that comes with make-up and clothes, because she retains the identity of the housewife. Her shopping for a pair of Nike shoes is an expression of affection for her daughter who covets a pair the couple can ill afford. Her entry is purely accidental, an accident which surprises all, since it defies every rule in the book of Indian middle class morality within and without marriage. Yet, without the surface make-up and gloss, director Basu Bhattacharya manages to make Mansi look as sensuous as possible, investing her persona with the seductiveness of an eroticised surface that implies something hidden, a secret or mystery.

But money is just a secondary bonus for Jaya, it is enjoyable also. She enjoys the secrecy and the sizzling sex that defines her job that needs her to serve a host of high-flying clients. She teaches herself tricks like swaying and gyrating her hips for a client in a white, translucent shirt over black hot pants or dressed up like a bride. This brings her as much entertainment as it does her clients. Somewhere along the line, it is clear that this is her prime source of happiness that her other life denied her. She cries in the shower when she learns that her husband is having fun on the side but does not even touch her in bed or out of it. We do not see her suffering from pangs of guilt. In fact, when the police raid the bordello, she forgets to hide her face like the other women do and raises her hands to cover her face only when it is too late.

Mansi in *Aastha* uses the professional experience she has been subtly tempted into, to enhance her sex life with her husband. Jaya's married life remains in the very stasis the film opened on. When Mansi's surprised husband asks her where she learnt tricks such as licking his ears during foreplay, with a soft smile, she says 'Blue films.'

The widespread control—broadly described as 'patriarchal'—of women's sexuality in the service of reproduction within the structure of marriage and family, renders other expressions of it as outlaw. But the 'illicitness' of prostitute-sex has to do more with the threat of non-productive sex: it is caused by the disapproval of commercial sex. This recognition allows us to locate prostitution within the ambit of the 'commercialisation of traditional female roles'—the reason for so much ambivalence in contemporary economics. When women place monetary value upon and claim payment for the work that they traditionally perform for 'free'—out of love, instinct, for intangible (non-monetary) 'rewards'—even outside the household, it is viewed as 'betrayal.'

Material deprivation has been portrayed as the main motive behind the entry of the heroine into the profession of a sex-worker in most films including *Aastha*. But in *Shaheb Bibi Golaam*, Gupta turns this theory on its head to show that sexual deprivation can produce the same result with similar consequences. Does this mean that women prioritise sex over motherhood? Not necessarily. But then, why should it matter to a patriarchal society if a woman enjoys both being an object of sexual pleasure for different men and being a consumer of sex with different men for a price—and at the same time enjoy the role-playing she has chosen for herself.

The outstanding, layered performance of Swastika Mukherjee as Bibi/Jaya/Shuktara makes the character much more meaningful than any other actress would have been able to make it not because other actresses are less talented but because Swastika can smoothly switch from Jaya to Shuktara and back. She does more than justice to the different dimensions of the character, aided by the costume designer and the make-up person. She has no inhibitions in doing any kind of scene or character or film and this helps in making the character both convincing and credible. Shuktara lays down her own conditions to the Madame. One, she would come in only during the day from Monday to Friday when her daughter is away at school. Two, she would retain the right to accept or reject a client. The Madam is flustered but gives in silently.

Though the distinctions between women who are prostitutes and women who are not are sharply and explicitly drawn in social negotiations and interactions, the slippages between the two categories are frequent and significant in theory, argument and practice. It is amusing therefore to even think that the regional board of the CBFC in eastern India could be so juvenile in thinking that showing a housewife doubling up as a prostitute is 'bad' for the audience! Of the two sides to her split personality, it should be interesting to find out which of the two is the impersonation and which is the real woman.

How Brutal Is Patriarchy?

QISSA (THE TALE of a Lonely Ghost), a feature film, exposes the shocking depths of insanity to which a father may be driven by his obsession with a male heir.

Qissa is an Arabic word which means 'folk tale.' The film presents a certain form of folk storytelling exemplified through tragic love legends like Heer-Ranjha, Laila-Majnu and so on. As in that form of narration, it gets into transgressions and interventions, sometimes unpredictable, sometimes open-ended, and sometimes closed.

'The story and script jointly done by Madhuja Mukherjee and me flows along and invites the audience to jump into the flow and participate in the story,' says director Anup Singh about *Qissa*. Singh, a FTII graduate was born in Dar-es-Salaam in Tanzania in a Punjabi Sikh family where his grandfather had migrated during the Partition. Their forced displacement is one of the main sources of inspiration for *Qissa*.

Placing the story of the film in a broader perspective, one can see a glimmer of the universal tragedy that Partition can bring about, not only in the lives of people affected by such geographical and political schisms but also in their ideology and their way of thinking.

Qissa, in fact, tells two stories of displacement. The first involves the forced displacement of Umber Singh (Irrfan Khan), a Sikh, and his family as a consequence of the religious violence following the Partition of India in 1947.

The second story of displacement is incredible in its inhumanity and brutality. It speaks of Umber Singh's manic obsession for a male heir to carry on his bloodline and how it wrecks the lives of his close ones, especially of Kanwar (Tilottama Shome), his fourth-born whose entire life is 'manufactured', manipulated, designed and dictated by her father's for a male heir.

Umber's wife Meher (Tisca Chopra) gives birth to three daughters. When she is pregnant for the fourth time, Umber Singh is confident that this time, she will deliver a boy. He remains present at the delivery, takes the new-born from the mother's lap and declares it is a boy.

'It would be better if you killed her,' cries his wife, in vain because she alone knows that the new-born is a girl. Umber convinces himself that the child is really a boy creating a tragic cage to trap himself in, never wanting to set himself free. How can he? He does not even know that he is caged within his obsession. Thus, the film reaches beyond Partition and folk tales to cross over to other areas of human psychology, of patriarchy strongly embedded in the mindset of the protagonist.

Does Kanwar know she is a girl? The film leaves this

question open till she is married off. Do Kanwar's sisters know that the little one is not their brother but their sister? Did Umber Singh bother to get his three daughters married? That too, remains hazy. These questions are suggested throughout the film but not answered, leaving the audience to draw its own conclusions.

Kanwar grows up under her fiercely protective father, confused about her identity—social, sexual and otherwise because she is kept distanced from her older sisters. To find out why, she sometimes peeps when one of them is bathing. Umber acquires the services of a wrestler to teach his youngest wrestling, who accepts everything without question, including the secret of her beginning to menstruate. Her father asks her not to tell her mother about this and the secret remains between father and daughter.

Kanwar grows up to become a truck driver and develops a fine camaraderie with her doting father who now wants to marry her off. Kanwar is attracted to Neeli, the daughter of the head of a gypsy group that sings and dances at weddings and festivals. Neeli likes Kanwar too and the two are married off and Umber Singh's carefully nurtured castle of secrets comes tumbling down.

Neeli and Kanwar still like each other but Neeli refuses to remain trapped in a marriage that will never be consummated. She tries to run away one night and a desperate Umber chases her and tries to rape her for that mandatory male heir that Kanwar cannot sire. Kanwar shoots him down and with her mother's help, the two run away to Meher's ancestral home in another village.

In the new place, a sisterhood is born between Kanwar and

Neeli. But much though Neeli tries to convert Kanwar into a girl, Kanwar finds it repulsive physically and mentally to fit into the new clothes, to leave her long hair loose, because she has been conditioned to grow up as a boy.

'When I wore that dress of yours, I felt as if scorpions were crawling all over me,' she says.

As curiosity among the new neighbourhood about Kanwar's gender and sex begins to escalate, Kanwar goes back to the village to bring back her mother but discovers that she died in a fire. One of her three sisters has lost her mind and is wandering around. Umber's ghost follows Kanwar back, intent on that male heir and Kanwar fails to rid herself of this ghost.

The film closes on a surrealistic note of magic realism where the identities of Umber and Kanwar merge into one and the stronger Umber overcomes and submerges the weak, vulnerable and perennially confused Kanwar within himself forever. Neeli, the most innocent of them all but also the strongest, looks on incredibly at this ghost of a man and jumps off the parapet of the ruins of the old home.

Qissa is a very dark film that moves from one dark area to the next, winding its way through the helpless, unhappy world the characters live in— Meher, the three daughters, but most importantly, the fiercely obsessed Umber and his hapless daughter, Kanwar. Neeli (Rasika Dugal) who finds she is married to a girl is the final victim of Umber's insanity.

Tilottama Shome as the grown Kanwar sustains restraint throughout her performance, her body language, her facial expression, her eyes spelling out the tragedy of her confused state. She is not only confused about her identity but also about her total surrender to her father's dictates, wanting to question but conditioned by training and discipline not to. This is perhaps the most extraordinary character any actress could have had the opportunity of essaying, and she has justified the director's choice and faith.

Irrfan Khan's multi-layered performance as Umber Singh, contrary to expectations, evokes more sympathy than hate. One is left with the question: Who, really, is the victim? Is it Umber Singh who loses everything and everyone because of his obsession or is it Kanwar, who has been conditioned to live out a gender she was not born into?

Or is it Meher, Umber's wife who realises that she is no more than a reproductive machine, expected to bear a son and when she cannot, she is forced to become a living witness to her daughter's tragedy. Neeli is also a victim for no fault of her own because she comes from a different background, a different society, a different culture.

Qissa was screened in the Contemporary World Cinema section at the 2013 Toronto International Film Festival where it bagged the prestigious Netpac Award for World/International Asian Film. It also won the Audience Choice Award at the International Film Festival, Rotterdam (IFFR) while Tilottama Shome won the Best Actress Award at the Abu Dhabi Film Festival for her role in the film. The film has been produced by Heimatfilm, Germany, Augustus Films, The Netherlands, and National Film Development Corporation, India.

The predominantly patriarchal misuse and abuse of medical technology for sex determination before a child is born, or aborting the foetus once it is known to be female, is not uncommon. But the deconstruction of the sex one is born into and reconstruction of the same child as male is something extremely rare. *Qissa* is an example of this belief translated to practice.

This involves no change in the genetic sex of the child but has deeper sociological, cultural and psychological ramifications for the person who is forced to go through this process without even knowing that under different historical-sociological circumstances, she might have had a choice.

Singh says he has heard of several such horrific stories in the northern parts of India, and was inspired by one particular story about a father who forced his teenage daughter to jump into the well during the riots—a common but brutal practice in Punjab before and during the Partition. For many years after the tragedy, this father was plagued by repeated nightmares of his dead daughter asking him 'Why?'.

RW Connell, a pioneer in developing a social theory of gender relations (*Gender and Power*, 1987) focusses on gender as a large-scale social structure and not just a matter of personal identity. Her work is concentric towards an exploration of what she calls 'hegemonic masculinity,' which is distanced from other masculinities, especially subordinated masculinities.

Hegemonic masculinity embodies the prevalent 'honour' and dominance associated with being a man and requires all other men to position themselves in relation to it. It ideologically legitimises the global subordination of women to men. So, we see in *Qissa* that even a strong and courageous woman like Meher is forced into silence and submission, not because she is scared of Umber but because she is concerned about the safety of all her daughters, including Kanwar.

The same logic applies to Neeli in a slightly different way. She is forced to stay on in her marital home even when she wants to go back to her group. She would have been raped by her father-in-law but it is Kanwar, a woman, who saves her even when it means shooting down her own father. The relationship between Neeli and Kanwar evolves into a warm sisterhood and companionship in the film, instead of predictably settling into a clichéd lesbian entanglement.

Even death does not liberate Umber Singh from his obsession for a male heir. The logic he presents is that after the Partition, there is no one left in his family to carry on the lineage. His warped ideology even legitimises incestual rape of his own daughter-in-law. This underscores the tragedy of the entire story—if keeping the lineage was the primary motive, then why was this little girl brought up as a boy when her father knew that she would never be able to sire a child?

But then again, did he even know? It does not seem so when one looks back at his life and observes how he taught himself to believe that Kanwar was his son, born a son and brought up as a son. True that *Qissa* is a Punjabi language film. But it carries a universal message that is very scary but also true.

Qissa leaves us with the question 'Can masculinity be manufactured?' The film seems to say that under the given time, space and paradigms where patriarchy reigns supreme—it can.

Films In Which Women Dominate

The film industry across the world is patriarchal. Though cinema is more than a hundred years old, its character has remained dominated by men—as directors, editors, actors, cinematographers, music directors, lyricists and so on. Most of the stories have men as the dominating character; women reflect their real-life situations as wives, mothers, lovers and daughters. Interestingly, the audience does not complain, including the women in it.

The tide seems to have turned since films with women in dominating roles began to make their presence felt. Names like Marlene Dietrich, Mae West, Katherine Hepburn and Greta Garbo come to mind as they dominated the frames of the films they featured in, sometimes in male masquerade—dressed up in male costumes but basically understood as women—or as characters with a negative slant, or as sexy females. Indian cinema has been less lucky in placing women in the centre of the narrative and cinematographic spaces of films.

Back home in India, a recent Bengali film *Onek Diner Pore* (After a Long Time) was released on a network website which has four women in lead roles and hardly any males worth talking about. The film is directed by Debarati Gupta, a woman filmmaker. The film is about four beautiful and daring women in their mid-thirties meeting at their school campus to reminisce about their good old schooldays. Recollections of the past bring out a few hidden dark tales of rivalries, insecurities and undercurrents beneath their 'almost perfect' friendship and life.

The director, who has made unusual feature films earlier, says, 'After my first movie, *Hoichoi,* this time I got the chance to tell my own story... to work in my own domain... And the absolute pleasure was to work with these wonderful actors! Swastika, Sudipta, Palomi and Rupanjana made my characters alive, real and more believable... As a writer and director I wanted to tell a story of my girlhood and womanhood. I am happy to see audiences are appreciating our efforts.' It is a reasonably well-knit film, with the four women demonstrating how childhood friends can grow up and progress quite differently from what their girlhood hinted at. The actresses seem emotionally invested in their characters and in the film itself, resulting in spontaneously natural performances. Of the four, one is a model-turned-actor (Palomi) and the other three are well established in acting.

The girl who stood first in class every time (Swastika) is now a middle-class housewife, quite happy and content as wife and mother in her small world with no regrets about how her life has progressed. The girl who had dreams of becoming a star in films (Rupanjana) is reduced to playing small parts and gets involved in the trafficking of young girls who want to make it in films. Palomi teaches at Stanford University in the US, is a single mother and leads a sexually permissive life. Sudipta portrays a gutsy single woman who cannot get rid of the bitterness resulting from a deeply abusive girlhood in her hostel and this comes across when the girls meet.

The film has a few men characters too who are marginalised but not given a negative slant, which is really commendable. It is not very 'empowering' but a well-made film that rises above mundane issues to tell a different story, helped greatly by wonderful performances.

Women-centric treatment can also be seen in Apanta Sen's latest feature film *Sonata*. It is in English, the language she chose for her directorial debut *36, Chowringhee Lane* more than 30 years ago. Sonata means 'a composition for an instrumental soloist, often with a piano accompaniment, typically in several movements with one or more in sonata form.' In this film, Beethoven's famous composition is used but the term also stands as a metaphor for the 'solo' lives of the three women taken in individually while the 'togetherness' is comprised in the 'accompaniment in several movements with one of more sonata form.'

Aparna explains, 'We do not have many films based on female bonding—the normal type without suggestions of alternative sex. I liked the changing moods and their interplay among these three women, each her own person, living life on her own terms and yet feeling close to the others. I wished to demolish the common belief that when two women get together, they are at each other's tooth and nail or sit down to have a gossip at the expense of others. I do not believe this is true. It happens but it is not a stereotype and I wanted to break this stereotype. *Sonata* is more an exploration of the feminine conscious than anything else,' says Aparna.

Sonata is the psychological exploration of three unmarried women facing a mid-life crisis: Aruna Chaturvedi (professor), Dolon Sen (sanker) and Subhadra Parekh (journalist) played by Aparna Sen, Shabana Azmi and Lillette Dubey respectively. The 103-minute film revolves around these three friends and their lives.

Sen is a master at expressing female bonding in the language of cinema and she breaks every rule in the cinema book to explore this in great depth through *Sonata*. The film is almost totally devoid of male presence except in a few snippety modes that are well edited. Youth is another market factor that is absent in this film. Sen excels in portraying three middle-aged women, two of whom live life entirely on their own terms and yet try to discover happiness and fulfilment in ways they choose.

Parched is a story about four women of different ages but similar geographical backdrops who find themselves trapped in diverse ways in a criminally patriarchal world. Are they aware of the tragedy of their lives? Will they continue to live within the pain and the humiliation till their deaths? The story unfolds with doses of fun, biting satire, humour, irony and a lot of sex and sexual innuendo.

Rani (Tannishtha Chatterjee), widowed at fifteen, is in her thirties and has a seventeen-year-old son Gulab (Riddhi Sen). Lajjo (Radhika Apte) is married to Madan, an alcoholic and a womaniser who uses sex with his wife not as a fulfilment of his physical hunger but as a weapon of torture. Janaki (Lehar

Khan) is childless and is punished for being so. At fourteen, she is married off to Gulab, for which Rani pays a dowry of Rs four lakh by mortgaging her small hutment. Bijlee (Surveen Chawla) is an item dancer in the touring circus that strikes tent in the village and also entertains customers at night for a fee.

This is a powerful feminist statement against patriarchy that defines a woman's life as a point of no return, never mind if she is a very young girl, a dancer-cum-sex worker, a widow or a married woman. The dialogue is full of sexual innuendo mainly indulged in by the women led by Bijlee, who performs on the most lovable item numbers one has seen on screen in a long time. The character is enriched by the sparkling performance of Surveen Chawla.

In one scene, she asks, 'Why should every expletive be prefixed by words like 'mother', 'sister'? Why should we not invent invectives and dirty expletives with men as prefixes such as 'fatherf.....r', 'brotherf....r' ourselves?' she asks, leading Rani and Lajjo to a hilltop where the three shout out their own expletives, a catharsis that gives them joy.

Lipstick Under My Burkha produced by Prakash Jha and directed by Alankrita Srivastava is a powerful political statement on how women can strategically use two extremely polarised women's items—the lipstick and the *burkha*—to articulate their sexual desires, irrespective of caste, class, age, community, faith and social status.

This film openly and without embarrassment explores not only women's sexuality but also the ingenuous and devious ways women try to fulfil their sexual and other desires clandestinely, using the veil to their advantage and the lipstick for their satisfaction in a way they *like* to and not because they are *forced* to. It won The Spirit of Asia award at the Tokyo International Film Festival and the Oxfam Award for Best Film on Gender Equality at the Mumbai International Film Festival.

Noted film critic Mythili Rao points out, *Lipstick Under my Burkha* does not get a censor certificate after it has done the festival rounds with a fair amount of success because 'the story is lady-oriented, their fantasy about life' and contains words of abuse and 'audio pornography.' The CBFC thinks that the semantic fudging of women into the more 'cultured' ladies justifies their decision. Pray, are ladies not women? They are not allowed fantasies—be it about life, including sex while mainstream cinema so often objectifies women to cater to male fantasies. Not just raunchy item numbers but discreet pandering to pious, so-called Indian values?'

The film is about how, even in a small-time city like Bhopal, with a mixed population of Hindus and Muslims living in harmony, four women are forced to lead double lives filled with a string of lies because of the socially conditioned patriarchal pressures they are oppressed by. These zero in mainly on their sexual fantasies and personal choice—in the form of dress, in choosing a profession she likes, in wanting to build a career and so on.

It is scathingly honest, it is sometimes scary, and it is a lot of fun too. The humour is as naturally structured into the script as is the satire and the scathing attack on the double standards of morality forced on intelligent, talented, spunky and creative women. You writhe in anger and you laugh at the *double entendre*s.

In all these women-centric film, you share the characters' pain and happiness.

Daughters Of Clay

DAUGHTERS OF CLAY is a short documentary conceptualised by JWT Kolkata and directed by Abhishek Sinha. The Bengali version *Kanya Rupeno* is a rare tribute to the creativity, courage and determination of three pioneers of Kumartuli, the nerve centre of sculpting Maa Durga and other Gods and Goddesses for Durga Puja and other festivals commissioned by people across the globe.

The film, released in 2017, showcases the journey of three women who braved apathy, ridicule and gender bias just to follow their hearts and make something out of their lives. They are the flag bearers of women power in Kumartuli today. The release on YouTube coincided with *Agomoni* or, the first day of *Debi Pakhsha* which also happens to be International Daughters' Day.

The film is anchored by famous Bengali litterateur Bani Basu who has won, among others, the Sahitya Academy Award.

She introduces us to three pillars of the Kumartuli artisan community—China Pal, Mala Pal and Kakoli Pal—who happen to be women. They talk about their struggles in this male-dominated cottage industry. Interestingly, the women stepped into the trade either due to circumstances or because they liked the artistry and the creativity involved, even though their fathers and husbands were against women entering this space.

China Pal was the youngest of six children. Her father did not like it one bit when he found her playing with clay as a child in his studio. He did not stop her from her enjoyment but did not back her either. 'My father passed away in 1994 and I decided to keep his old studio running because there were commissioned orders to be fulfilled. Besides, I loved the challenge of stepping into a man's world and of creating different models of different Goddesses myself. There were many who discouraged me, saying it was a man's job and asked me to sell off the studio. But I was determined to keep it running and now, I have a full-fledged workshop working almost round the clock just before the festival season begins,' she says.

'My father was renowned for his *Ekchala Thakurs* (*Ekchala* means Mother Goddess, her children, Asura and the lion all placed under a single arch) and I have followed his tradition,' she adds.

Nemesis played a decisive role in Kakoli Pal's life, forcing her to join the idol-making fold. 'I was forbidden to even step inside a studio or play with clay dolls which was the fate of all daughters born into the family of idol makers. I never dared to dream that I would become a much-in-demand artisan one day. But it came in the wake of a tragedy. My husband Asim Pal, suddenly passed away just the day after Lakshmi Puja in

2003. The commissioned work had to be finished and my two growing daughters had to study and my life changed forever,' says Kakoli, wiping a tear in memory of her husband. 'The studio has been my home and my abode of peace and creativity. I have expanded the business. My husband could barely manage to create five to seven idols, I have been commissioned this year to deliver 22 idols of the Goddess,' she sums up.

Slim and dusky Mala Pal wears a sad expression on her face. She was very fond of making small, crude figurines out of wet clay. Her father did not quite care for her way of spending her spare time. 'But my elder brother Kalu da felt differently. He not only taught me the finer nuances of the art but became my mentor and encouraged me to follow my passion honestly. After father passed away in 1985, I decided to run his studio all by myself. Many of my peers in Kumartuli, all men, resisted my entry into the art and business of this work but I was determined to go ahead and create something that would stand the test of time in my life,' she says. Customers who once deserted her studio only because they did not trust her as she was a woman, came back and her business grew rapidly. She concentrates on miniature idols of all Goddesses in the Hindu pantheon in the Bengali tradition and they are shipped to cities like Delhi, Bengaluru and Mumbai and beyond Indian shores to countries such as US, Canada, Germany and Dubai.

The only time we see Mala smiling in the film is when she puts on the gold chain gifted to all the three women by PC Chandra Jewellers. Though this five-minute film is an ad film, its social agenda of paying tribute to the invisible women clay idol makers in Kolkata is commendable. Of course, five minutes is too short for this kind of tribute. Besides, there are several other women clay idol makers in the business today.

Namita Pal is based in Potopara near Kalighat which is like another Kumartuli in miniature. Shipra Ghodui and Shibani Pal have their work units in Andul, some distance from Kolkata.

Each Durga 'family'—Durga, her four children, Mahisasura and the Lion—takes around two months to complete and is priced within a range of Rs 10,000 to Rs 2 lakh. Orders from abroad must be completed and shipped by April-May mainly through reputed couriers. They are packed in boxed made of ply shaped like cupboards and locked for security.

'We work with cement, plaster, bronze and copper because public tastes are ever-evolving. A truckload of sand now costs more than Rs 2,000 while wet clay is priced approximately above Rs 800 per truckload. Clubs and collective organisations that place orders for idols often slip up when it is payment time. Many of them scoot off when we ask for payment. So, I have settled for family *puja* orders because they are very good paymasters in terms of time,' says China Pal.

The rising price and declining supply of raw materials, constant and frequent power cuts, lack of space, lack of working capital and labour problems plague the idol-makers. 'I generally take orders from 20 parties every year, and sometimes it crosses this mark. But the only way I can raise funds to begin my work is by raising loans from friends and relatives. I ran up a loan of Rs 45,000 in 2004 and my nephews chipped in. Otherwise, I would have been in the red,' says Shibani Pal. Forty-six-year-old Namita Pal says that labour rates have risen. 'But I cannot turn them down even when they are charging Rs 300-400 per day because the workers have become a part of my family,' she says. 'Every year, I tell myself, this is the last time I will do business in clay idols. I will have to find out something else next year with the expertise, experience and skill I have gained. But as January approaches and orders for Saraswati idols begin to come in, I forget the resolution and get caught up in the web of orders, creation and tension,' says Shibani.

Namita, Shibani and Shipra are not in this film and perhaps, several others who continue to be victims of the invisibility that women are vulnerable to. Maybe another year, another documentary will fill in this vacuum.

Sex Or Gender?

NO OTHER INDIAN feature film has touched upon a subject like sex reassignment surgery undergone by a man to become a woman except *Chitrangada – The Crowning Wish*, written and directed by noted filmmaker Rituparno Ghosh which tackles this issue head-on through the eyes of its protagonist Rudra Chatterjee enacted by Ghosh himself.

Rudrajit is a dancer-choreographer who is in the process of choreographing Rabindranath Tagore's dance drama *Chitrangada* to celebrate the bard's 150 birth anniversary. He is gay and develops a strange relationship with replacement drummer Partho, who is a drug addict.

Why does Rudra decide on this complex series of surgeries to change his sex? He discovers that Partho is very fond of children. As the law proscribes adoption by two men sharing a love relationship, Rudra does not want Partho to regret not having children so he decides they must adopt one. The surgery is a long-term, delicate and complex process that has deep emotional and psychological repercussions not only on the person undergoing the surgeries but also on the people he is closely related to such as his parents, his colleagues in the dance troupe, his friends and most importantly, his lover.

Sex Reassignment Rurgery (SRS) from male to female involves reshaping the male genitals with the appearance of and, as far as possible, the function of female genitalia. Prior to any surgeries, trans-women usually undergo hormone replacement therapy and facial hair removal. Other surgeries undergone by trans-women may include facial feminisation. These usually begin with breast implants and end with vaginal reassignment.

Lili Elbe was the first known recipient of male-to-female SRS in Germany in 1930, a process that involved five surgeries. However, she died three months after her fifth operation. The first male-to-female surgeries in the United States took place in 1966 at the Johns Hopkins University Medical Center. The first physician who performed sex reassignment surgeries in the US was the late Dr Elmer Belt. He stopped doing these surgeries in the late sixties.

The aesthetic, sensational and functional results of the many surgeries within SRS vary greatly. Surgeons differ considerably in their techniques and skills; patients' skins vary in elasticity and healing ability (affected by smoking for example), previous surgeries in the given areas, and complications resulting from problems such as infections, blood loss or nerve damage. However, in the best cases, when recovery from surgery is complete, it is difficult for anyone to detect that someone has undergone SRS.

Chitrangada, however, has a slightly different story to tell, rather, several different stories. The lines between Rituparno as performer on screen and Rituparno as the man away from screen get blurred as the film keeps leaning on the Tagore story picked from an episode of the *Mahabharata* to rationalise Ritu/Rudra's struggles—not only with the sex he is born with and into, but also the sex he wants to change into. Rituparno in real life is reportedly transgender by choice and has undergone a number of surgeries. Rudra goes through the process of *becoming* a woman but is never sure whether he is doing it to have a fulfilling life with Partho or because he is unhappy in the sex he was born into.

It also does not occur to him to question that the long gaps in his close association with Partho, because of the surgical procedures, might create a deep dent in a relationship that was just getting built. He does not consider that a drug addict might also be fickle enough to turn to the first person—this time a woman—to fall for and ditch him unceremoniously. Ghosh the filmmaker says that the film explores the right of a person to choose his/her sex in a world where everything is in a state of constant flux. But is Rudra really making a 'choice' or is he veiling his confusion with 'choice'?

Ghosh says, 'This is a changeable world. Nothing is permanent—possessions, love, things we own, even our own bodies. Why do we then cling to things like gender and identity with such fierceness? Why do we turn them into such issues? *Chitrangada* is Tagore's exploration into the reality of identity. It asks the question—who are we, really?'

Does a surgical transition from male to female essentially bring about associated changes in one's gender? *Chitrangada* fails to explore this distinction. But SRS is purely a question of medical anatomical transformation. Sociologists and feminists insist that sex is purely a biological fact over which outside factors have no control. SRS has proved otherwise. But this does not change in any way the fact that gender is socio-cultural and environmental. It is determined continuously throughout the growth and development of the individual's life. 'Sex' determines maleness and femaleness, both of which are based purely on physical and anatomical differences. 'Gender' determines masculinity and femininity, both of which are based on cultural differences.

In this film, as its protagonist and as a person himself, Ghosh fails to see this basic difference between sex and gender and works on the assumption that a change in 'sex' through surgeries will automatically bring about a change in the 'gender' associations he thinks he has. Does he? This remains unanswered till the film closes with his request to his surgeon to cancel the last vaginal surgery and also to reverse the entire process he has already gone through. Does he do this because Partho is not interested in a 'synthetic' woman and would love to get back the old Rudra? Or, does he do this because he is really no longer sure whether he wants a complete sex change or not?

Feminists have delineated the difference between 'sex' and 'gender' in order to dissociate the cognition of sex from its cultural implications. Feminist scholar Maithreyee Krishnaraj says, 'Terminology is not a meaningless sophistication. Non-Marxist theories have done extensive analysis (commonly denoted by the idea of sex roles) on how gender is psycho-socially constructed. Psychoanalysis and feminism owe debts to each other.' In what way does *Chitrangada* address this issue? The answer is simple—it does not. The exaggerated form of conditioned and cliché effeminate behaviour one finds in Rudra—talking in soft whispers, the graceful movement of hands, the body language in repose and in dance, are reflective of the way Rituparno Ghosh behaves in real life.

The constant referring back to Tagore's *Chitrangada* does not establish Ghosh's theory. Chitrangada, a Manipuri princess, was brought up by her father like a son. When Arjuna sees her for the first time, he takes her for a young man and turns away. But she falls in love with him at first sight and asks Madana, the God of Love, to transform her into a beautiful woman. He grants her this wish but only for a year. Arjuna and the transformed Chitrangada now enjoy emotional togetherness till Arjuna tires of her beauty and hearing about the brave feats of the original Chitrangada in male garb, wants to meet her in person. The beautiful Chitrangada asks Madana to reverse the boon. Chitrangada and Arjuna lead a happy life and even beget a son till Arjuna goes into exile. The imaginatively designed abstracts from the performance of Tagore's *Chitrangada* within the film are not pure and diluted Tagore and at best, they remain ambivalent and present modern mutations and fusions of Tagore.

The only common link between Rudra's and Chitrangada's experience is that both want to go back to what they were acculturised to be. But while Chitrangada is happy to rule Manipur after her father's demise without Arjuna beside her, we know for certain that Rudra's love story ends on a tragic note of uncertainty.

Run Kalyani

RUN KALYANI IS one-time film journalist J Geetha's directorial debut. The feature film reveals how a deceptively simple storyline can enrich the tapestry of life—on celluloid and in real life.

J Geetha started as a print journalist, later moving to television. On acquiring her own video camera, she made her first film *Woman with a Video Camera* (2005) from Kerala, a state that had hardly any woman filmmaker then. Geetha then founded AkamPuram, an independent production company that has a distinctive slate of films to its credit. Geetha received the Göteborg International Film Festival's Development Fund for her first script *A Certain Slant of Light* (2008).

However, lack of funding for feature fiction only meant a focus on writing scripts and a return to documentaries as producer. She attended the Berlin Talent Campus in 2009. Her second script *End Game* was at the Co-Production Market in

2014 at Film Bazaar. *Run Kalyani* is her debut feature fiction set in Trivandrum, Kerala, and was part of the *Work in Progress Lab* in 2018 at Film Bazaar. It won the Special Jury Prize at the 25th Kolkata International Film Festival recently. Her debut film *Run Kalyani* drew a packed house when a special screening was held in her native city, Thiruvananthapuram.

The young woman protagonist lives with her aunt in a rundown *Agraharam* in Thiruvananthapuram. The *Agraharam* is a tenanted small two-storey, self-contained apartment. Her aunt, once a dancer, is now paralysed and bedridden and has lost her power of speech. Kalyani is very fond of this aunt and tends to her like any mother would. After this, Kalyani leaves to cook food for two households close to where she lives. These two families form two interesting sub-plots and also evolve a common link that offers hope to Kalyani and distress to one of the families.

Talking about her motivation in making the film, Geetha says: 'I have seen women who work so hard but are shadowy figures and live an unseen life. But is their life really any less dramatic? Do they really live a life of no agency? No. And through Kalyani's eyes we see many other women and men. This is not a polarised film about men and women. It is about all of us, trapped in a pattern of living, but life is never static. It keeps changing and we have to be alert to that and make the right intervention. It is like a game of chess, really!'

Since Kalyani is a cook by profession, the camera and editing focus a lot on different processes of cooking that function like an editing strategy and mark a movement of the film from point A to point B to point C. Kalyani chopping vegetables, roasting onions and red chilllies strung on a tiny *seekh* and dipping them in a pot full of curry, Kalyani baking fresh *idlis* for her aunt and placing them neatly on a side table beside her bed, Kalyani serving her employers and so on which also offers an insight into her perfectionism and a good diversion from the main story. The difference in the menu among the three houses, which includes Kalyani's own are also very suggestive of their respective lifestyles and eating habits. The minute detailing not only of objects but also of the characters—big and small—is incredible.

Kalyani is quite reserved and the only place she opens up is when she is talking to her aunt and a would-be young film director who keeps writing absurd scripts but never finishing them. He appears to live on the upper floor anteroom of the home where Kalyani lives. But we never see him stepping out of the room or the house, so one may safely assume that this is Geetha's touch of surrealism to an otherwise simple story. Kalyani rests in this room and is unimpressed by his unfinished scripts and smiles at them or just goes to sleep. This director is certainly a figment of her ingenuous imagination.

Kalyani and her aunt have a heavy debt burden, including arrears in rent, electricity bill and so on. She also has to fend off a persuasive marriage proposal which is not to her liking but we can see her taking some money through the door probably as an 'incentive' to tempt her to marriage. A driver of the multi-storey apartment complex she works in tries to attract her attention every day but fails and gives up.

Her regular walk to the homes she works in and back to her own home is followed faithfully by the camera. A deranged man dressed in white delivers nonsensical lecture from morning to evening both in Malayalam and English while he walks across the road and back. There is another man who is constantly playing on a *nadaswaram* under a huge banyan tree. Kalyani likes the music and her gait slows down, her eyes turn dreamy as she reaches near the tree and then perks up again.

The two families Kalyani cooks for have their own issues. One is a joint family comprised of a patriarch who constantly plays chess and uses competitive chess terms as he plans his moves. He has two sons, one extremely henpecked with a snobbish wife and the other, who beats up his ex-surgeon wife, seems slightly mentally unstable. Kalyani does not interact with them at all unless she needs to.

Geetha says, 'There are probably many issues embedded in the pattern of the film that may be picked up by viewers. Firstly, the film is about families and the secret problems they hide, such as domestic violence. The film is about women, women with dreams, desire, duties. It is about class too, here the Brahmin working class! It is about care for the elderly and total lack of State support or community support for the same. It is about retirement age, as able and experienced employees have to retire in their mid-fifties. It is about love, not just amongst the youth but amongst the mature adults too. It is about youth and fanciful dreams. It is about the inner strength that Kalyani possesses. It is about a place, shot as it is entirely in Thiruvananthapuram.'

Geetha has also captured the changing architectural space of the city, where we can see walls covered not only with graffiti but also with paintings and drawings of once-famous celebrities like Kamala Das, Kavalam Narayana Panickar, and so on. The music is distinguished by the change in rhythm with the change in Kalyani's movement from her workplace and back.

As she walks down the complex, some percussion instruments can be heard, which changes to the *nadasawaram* (trumpet) as she approaches the musician under that big banyan tree. He keeps aside his instrument when Kalyani walks back towards the end.

According to Geetha, '*Run Kalyani* is an ensemble drama with equally important male and female characters. However, the women characters signify something more, right from the lead Kalyani to her aunt Rukmini, the two women in the house where she goes to cook and the visiting daughter of the house. When films nowadays including the "feminist" and the "art house" are all becoming shrill and aggressive, I want to seek the steely strength that women have and bring that to life. Kalyani is an amazing character—she is gentle, quiet, caring but is also made of something stronger and is a survivor.'

Garggo Anantham as Kalyani is outstanding in a very low-key but confident and dignified performance which deserves an award. The script does not give Kalyani, her aunt or anyone else any back story yet the story moves on without jerks.

The closure is a bit of a commercial compromise but it is in harmony with the rest of the film and comes as a pleasant surprise. One wonders if the magic realism really belongs to the film and could have been edited out. But then, the director has her own ideas. Old-timer Madhu, who is one of the best-known actors of his time, makes a surprising appearance in a cameo as a chess-crazy old man not bothered about the squabbles going on around him. Meera Nair as Nirmala, the slightly mentally disturbed ex-surgeon is good but why she wears the same sari in every scene except one is a mystery because the family is very affluent. Swati Premji as Sonali's supine aunt is very expressive and does much more with her face than with her body.

Run Kalyani is a film that defines freedom in a different way, touching fine emotions with finely nuanced touches and is a brilliant debut indeed.

Ajji
A Mirror To System

AJJI IS A film that shocks. Through an ideal marriage between form and content, equipped with the infrastructural back-up of cinematography, editing, sound effects, music and acting, the rich tapestry is devoid of glamour, chutzpah, romance and everything expected from a film. Devashish Makhija's second feature film is like a virtual slap on your complacent face. A face that belongs to all of us who cluck our tongues sadly when we watch candlelight marches on our television screens demanding justice for a rape victim and forget all about it once the news channel turns to another report on the inhumanity of man against man.

The film produced by Yoodle Films was screened at the Indian Film Festival at Los Angeles. Actress Sushama Deshpande, who played the title role, received a Special Jury mention for her performance in the film and also The Flame Award at the UK Asian Film Festival. The film also won the

Fresh Blood competition at the Beune International Thriller Festival, 2018. Among other marks of recognition and festival screenings are: official selection at the 2017 Busan International Film Festival, showcasing in the New Currents Section of the 22 Korean Film Extravaganza and nomination for the Oxfam Best Film on Gender Equality Award category at the 19 Mumbai Film Festival 2017.

Ajji means granny in Marathi. Ajji, around 65, is grandmother to ten-year-old Manda, who fails to return from Ajji's customer's house where she had gone to deliver some tailored clothes. When Ajji along with Manda's parents go looking for her in the pitch dark of night, they find her lying in a ditch, battered and bruised. Manda has been raped and cannot even speak, let alone rise from her bed. As the family is afraid of summoning a doctor, she continues to bleed round the clock and is administered indigenous ointments bought from a local woman.

When the local cop comes to 'investigate' it is only to warn them against filing a FIR that may get them into trouble because they are involved in an 'illegal' trade and more importantly, because the rapist Dhawale is the son of the powerful local councillor. Manda's parents are terrified and refuse to file an FIR against Dhawle as they fear repercussions.

The policeman, visibly relieved, leaves the scene and is angry when Ajji tells him to write down the complaint and file a FIR. It seems as if Ajji is stunned by an electric shock worse than the debris of her life. The rapist is known for raping minors, workers on his construction sites and Dalit women but is never punished, thanks to the greedy policeman who is treated like a slave by Dhawle. The victim's pain does not seem to dissipate at all and yet we, along with the characters in the film, can do nothing but watch helplessly.

Rape in Indian cinema is used mainly as a technologically skilled manipulation used imaginatively for purely commercial purposes. But Makhija staunchly refuses to create the space for visual pleasure because the actual rape is never shown. It is the *impact* of rape, mainly on the little girl who innocently asks her granny whether she has finally grown up or not, and the granny that become the focus of the camera, the sound design and the narrative. The magic lighting alternating between dark and brightness on her wrinkled face show her anger and incredulity.

Held in tight close-ups, her face is filled with myriad expressions that reveal her anger at herself for not being able to help Manda, anger at the police for its corruption and sycophancy, anger at her own son and daughter-in-law for not seeking medical help for their abused daughter and anger at Dhawle. She begins to spy on him in the darkness of night when everyone at home is fast asleep.

Ajji visits the local butcher who is her friend, though the family is vegetarian. Her demand is chilling. "Teach me to butcher cows and cut them into beef and sheep to slice and turn into meat," she tells him. He says that Muslim women are not allowed to do this so how can a Hindu woman learn the skill of butchering? But the old lady is adamant and says she will not budge from his shop unless he teaches her. So, between her daily chores of applying ointment to Manda's painful sores and tailoring clothes, Ajji begins earnestly to learn the fine skill of butchery, swallowing her disgust but not allowing herself to be overpowered by it.

Ajji (Sushama Deshjpande) converts her aim of destroying

the rapist into a learning experience she may never have imagined in her entire life. The most outstanding feature of her character is her tremendous courage, unfettered by terrible arthritis, age, poverty, mental stress due to her grand-daughter's condition. She braces herself and preps carefully to operationalise her plans. From her clandestine espionage, the audience also peeps into the bizarre ugliness of Dhawale's perversion, especially in a scene where he is disfiguring and dismembering a mannequin, his way of enjoying sex till, at the end of the act, the camera focusses for a minute on the severed head staring blankly into space. This scene is as bizarre as it is disturbing and may also be read as a vicarious projection.

The fabrication of the female body, the play of skin and make-up, nudity and dress, the constant recombination of organs, construction of the representational space by depth of field, diffractions of light, and colour effects—in short, the process of fabrication of the film from decoupage to montage. This is a scene longer than it ought to be, investing the film with perverse voyeurism it should have done without, even if it is meant to highlight the primal nature of Dhawale.

Dark goggles worn by both Dhawale and his father are used as symbols of power, their subconscious way of hiding their crimes with the darkness that the glares provide and probably invest them with some amount of anonymity for their own protection. The performances appear to organically flow out of the actors, every single one of them, led by Ajji and the main perpetrator Dhawle. The art direction is minutely detailed: the shanty's blue walls, a family picture, vessels, a small cooking place, Ajji's sewing machine, the dull and overused clothes worn by the characters. That touch of Ajji feeding the street dogs with the meat she cuts on the first day, as also when Leela paints Ajji's face with thick make-up, are truly moving.

Setting aside this torturous scene, Manda cringing in endless pain, trying to get close to her father for some consolation, highlights the tragedy of being poor, vulnerable and helpless in the face of a criminal who wields power because the system is corrupt and is more than willing to look the other way in exchange for money and other favours. There is no attempt to sensationalise the drama nor any melodramatic touches of chest-beating or wailing or crying when the girl is brought home, which is also a powerful metaphor for the silence marginalised people have turned into a way of life to protect themselves from further humiliation, insult and torture.

Leela (Sadiya Siddique) secretly helps Ajji in some of her endeavours and throws up an interesting cameo. She is their neighbour, a pregnant prostitute who has no a clue of what Ajji is contemplating and why. She is nursing a fellow sex worker who has been another victim Dhawale because she refused his demand for sex.

The climax has a drunken Dhawale tottering down dark alleyways with Ajji following him, the tables turned. He does not even know that he is being stalked with a purpose by someone physically weaker, chronologically older and a woman who one cannot even imagine to be the perpetrator of a murder. Can and does this justify Ajji's well-planned, calculating and diabolic revenge plan? Or does this place her at Dhawale's level? This raises several questions of right and wrong, what is morally justified and what is not. But when the system in which Ajji, her son out of a job after an accident in the workplace, Manda and Leela live in, is corrupt, corroded and diseased with the law, the administrative and the judicial machinery even at the slum level completely compromised, can one truly stand on judgement on the wronged woman like Ajji?

Every man, woman and child is capable of anything he/she puts her mind to, never mind the lines that divide us in terms of age, education, health, place, language, financial status and class. This is the basic foundation on which the script of *Ajji* is built. The basic philosophy is not only the attack on corruption, crime and power but also sheds light on the way these three socio-political evils, personified in Dhawale, are manipulated to pay the price for their evil deeds through the same device that marks them as evil in the first place.

Thappad
A Slap On Society

THAPPAD MEANS 'SLAP.' It means just what it is in its physical sense. In this film, it means a sudden, unannounced slap a husband lands on his wife's fair cheek in the middle of a house party in the presence of invitees, family members and household domestic. But the echoes of this slap resound right through the film pointing out how, placed in an urban Indian metro within a loving family at the present time, a slap can shake the very foundations of a seemingly happy marriage with the couple looking forward to a bright future in a new house with a blue door in faraway London.

Anubhav Sinha's *Mulk* explored with the sharpness of a knife the victimisation of a Muslim family innocent of any involvement in a terrorist attack. *Article 375* underscored the lackadaisical and corrupt practices within the legal and judicial machinery in dealing with the rape and murder of two Dalit girls committed by a high caste local politician and a couple of police staff.

The husband (Pavail Gulati) is shocked much more by his wife's reaction to the slap than the fact that he actually executed the slap! He takes her quiet anger as an over-reaction because patriarchy has taught him to internalise that a husband's slapping of his wife is no big deal. His mother and even Amrita's mother and brother feel the same way. 'Move on' they urge her, put the slap behind you. But the otherwise dutiful, responsible, perfect housewife Amrita begins to retrospect on the past and introspect on the present, her shock driving her into the silent mode when all she can tell her husband is 'I don't love you anymore. How can I live with you then?'

Amrita has the makings of an icon of perfection as she lives out her everyday life having happily quit her promising career as a dancer. Some consolation comes in the form of Kathak lessons she gives to her neighbour's daughter. She wakes up earlier than her husband who has set the alarm, picks the milk and the newspaper from the doorstep, snips the plants at the window sill, checks the sugar level of her mother-in-law (Tanvi Azmi), makes herself a cup of green tea and waits for Vikram to escort him to the car with his flask of coffee, his cellphone and his wallet. She is happy with her life and with the dream of the London home with that blue door. The slap changes all that and her world crashes around her feet.

Vikram too has internalised, consciously or subconsciously, the patriarchal theory that a husband can do whatever he wants with his wife and an occasional slap is just a 'small thing' which happens to all wives. He is shocked at his docile wife's refusal to mend bridges and her leaving to stay with her parents 'for some time at least.' Her brother is also shocked at her intention to walk out of what he felt was 'an ideal marriage.' But her brother's fiancée Swati backs Amrita all the way and this brings a schism in the relationship between the younger couple. Amrita's mother (Ratna Pathak) is aghast but her father (Kumud Mishra) who addresses his wife with the respectful 'Aap' stands staunchly behind his daughter—till his wife reminds him that he never asked her whether she liked giving up music when she married.

The beautiful neighbour (Dia Mirza) is a widow and cannot imagine marrying again as her husband was too precious to be replaced. When Amrita approaches Nethra (Maya Sarao), a matrimonial lawyer who sits in her famous father-in-law's chambers, the lawyer begins to look at her own marriage to a hot-shot star journalist (Manav Kaul), an arrogant man who never forgets to remind her that she owes her success to inheriting his now-paralytic father's practice and also to his own fame as a journalist. This man has no clue that his wife is having a torrid affair with a much kinder and humane young chef who understands her perfectly and gives her the space she needs. Eventually, Nethra walks out of it all, including the affair, because she wants to start life afresh.

Sumitra, the skeletal domestic who works in Amrita's house, is beaten up so badly by her horrible husband on a daily basis that one day, she finally takes a knife and challenges him to kill her. When he does not, she beats him up till he backs off, scared to see this new wife. Sumitra is fed up of being abused for being 'barren'; she keeps telling her husband to go for a fertility test himself.

This is essentially a character-driven story, with each character fleshed out to add a new dimension to the narrative honed to near perfection by every single actor whose performance is so organic that you begin to believe that they are real. This is topped by Taapsi Pannu, who has been enacting out-of-the-box roles in almost all her films. A telling comment she makes on her present situation is when she tells her lawyer, 'Maybe I brought this insult on myself, who knows?' The second and more significant comment is when she says she suddenly realises that yellow is her favourite colour, so how is it that she was always dreaming of a *blue* door?

Ram Kapoor stands out in a brief cameo as the lawyer from Vikram's side. The music is okay but songs, even on the soundtrack, are superfluous in this film. Maya Sarao as the lawyer excels as the outwardly super confident successful lawyer but a slightly scared and confused woman inside. The opening scenes when she pushes her head out of the car window to allow the breeze to kiss her face is stunning, specially for what follows. The cinematography is brilliant and so are the sound effects—Amrita pushes back the furniture on the morning after the party night and the noise conveys to us that perhaps she is trying to rearrange her life back to the way it was before she was married. Vikram is perhaps more devastated than Amrita because the wife has great amounts of inner strength she draws from while the husband does not.

Thappad is not about domestic violence, as its title may indicate. It is rather, a critique of patriarchy in the subtlest manner where a husband's slapping of his wife, in public or in private, planned or in the heat of the moment, humiliates and insults not just the victim but also the victimiser. It shows him up as less than a human being because though he is shocked that his wife wants to leave home, it never occurs to him to apologise to her for his behaviour. By the time he realises this, it is already too late. The slap is a reminder for the wife Amrita (Taapsi Pannu) that her position as wife, daughter-in-law and so on is more a put-on than she ever imagined. Her name which means 'immortality' is as much a lie as her life is. The same applies to the husband whose name Vikram means 'valour'.

The film reminds us of Henrick Ibsen's *A Doll's House* first staged in 1879. It still remains one of the most widely performed plays across the world. It shook the European world because of the very unpredictable and radical climax when Nora slams the door and walks out on her husband and three kids, never to come back. This went radically against patriarchal norms that dominated society at that time. Like it or not, they still do.

Even though, *A Doll's House,* created as a direct attack on the institution of marriage and its discrimination between the husband and the wife, Ibsen insisted that he never wanted to talk about the mistreatment of women but about discrimination between and among all humans. In a speech, Ibsen insisted that he 'must disclaim the honour of having consciously worked for the women's rights movement,' since he wrote 'without any conscious thought of making propaganda,' his task having been 'the description of humanity.'.

However, the character of Amrita is depicted in a slightly melodramatic mode revealed in the puja scene when she returns home in reverence to her mother-in-law's request and carries on an unending monologue dressed almost like a bride. This takes much of the sting off her walkout. At the same time, Sinha manages to convey that much to our belief to the contrary, most women would think more than twice before leaving home and hearth, husband and children to live life on their own terms. The entire society and family she lives in, reminds her again and again that she should not leave home and 'these are just small things all women face and bear with.' Often, she brings it upon herself.